Divorce Dog
Men, Motherhood and Midlife

Kim McLarin

DIVORCE DOG

Uncle Jimmy Books

ISBN-10: 0692456902
ISBN-13: 978-0692456903

DEDICATION

For James Baldwin, who saved my life. And for Samantha and Isaac, who saved it some more.

DIVORCE DOG

CONTENTS

DIVORCE DOG

ACKNOWLEDGMENTS

I'm grateful to the children, and to Beth, Jackie, Bridgit, Susan and other sister-friends who keep me relatively sane. To my family of birth and my family of faith at Union United Methodist Church in Boston. To God. And to James Baldwin.
All quotes from *James Baldwin: Collected Essays*. Library of America. February 1998

DIVORCE DOG

FASTING FOR OJ

A few years ago I walked into the family room of my mother's house to find her sitting on the couch, hands in her lap, silently drenched in tears.

"What's wrong?" I asked, startled.

She sobbed out loud then, no longer contained and very quickly the sobs increased in volume and degree. "I'm hurt!" she cried, over and over. As though she'd been sitting there waiting for someone to come along and notice, to stop and witness her pain.

"I'm hurt, I'm hurt, I'm hurt."

Because I wasn't listening carefully these words at first brought a kind of relief. My mother had recently been diagnosed with stage IV colon cancer and we were all suddenly engaged in the fierce battle to save her life. I'd flown from Boston to California for an extended weekend, temporarily leaving my children and my own crumbled marriage/ life behind to take my turn at the cancer wheel. Already I'd escorted her to her chemotherapy appointment, had sat in the oncologist's office and tried to translate his medical jargon to her and her alternately submissive and obstructionist responses to him. Already I'd stroked and thanked the woman living at the house to help out. Already I'd gone Costco shopping in search of something my mother could eat or drink to keep up her strength. Already I'd sat with my mother in the emergency room all though Saturday night and into Sunday morning, waiting for someone to disconnect the chemo pump making her intolerably sick. Already I'd witnessed this weak and diminished version of the woman who'd loomed over my childhood like an avenging angel. This was just more of the same.

"What hurts?" I demanded. Identify the problem. Identify the problem properly and it can usually be resolved. Or so I wanted to believe.

"Tell me and I'll call the nurse."

"I'm hurt." Her whole body shook. I'd seen my mother cry before but still it's never easy, spotting the hairline cracks in the foundation of one's life. I'd seen my mother cry before but never like this, never so helplessly and absent of hope. My mother tends to channel her pain and frustration into anger rather than sadness. I take after her in that way.

"Let's go to the clinic," I urged, already moving to the door. "I'll call on the way but let's go now, before it gets too late and we have to go to the emergency room."

My mother did not move. "I'm hurt."

That time I heard her: not *"It hurt"* or *"I'm hurting"* but "I'm hurt." I am injured or wounded. I am damaged and in pain.

This made me furious.

I bristled, stood before her with my hands on my hips like a jerk. "You're depressed," I told her.

"Nobody ever loved me."

Did I roll my eyes? Did I actually roll my eyes? Probably. But she didn't see because she was still staring downward. "You're depressed and I've been telling you that. The doctor has been telling you that. You need to go see somebody."

That raised her. "No." Then, more sobbing. "I'm hurt."

And so it went for awhile, my mother sobbing and injured, me increasingly furious. I was angry not because I didn't believe her—if there's anybody I know who has the right to sit and sob about their pain it's certainly she. I was angry because after a lifetime of struggling to understand my mother, after a long and winding trail that began in desperate love, moved to anger, swept to guilt, stumbled to appeasement and then back to guilt I thought I'd finally settled on a category in which to place the most perplexing person I've ever known: she was depressed. My mother was depressed and always had been and now the cancer treatment had made things worse, had only intensified what was already there. That explained everything!

Only she wouldn't go along.

"I'm not crazy, I'm hurt," my mother sobbed, not moving. "Why is that so hard to understand?"

A reasonable question. One which has dominated my life.

**

Here's a little story to start, one about my mother, one that begins to explain why I always struggled to explain her. OJ Simpson. Remember him?

Remember that strange and polarizing trial? Remember that watershed acquittal that shocked—shocked! —and outraged so many (white) Americans and therefore, for the very same reasons, delighted so many black Americans? My mother danced.

My mother danced but hers was no idle jubilation; she'd earned her happiness at the verdict, earned it by fasting and praying on OJ's behalf for months. I know because she told me, late in the game, after we'd already declared our various positions and agreed to disagree and gone on. It just came up one day, out of the blue: "I'm fasting for OJ," she said.

I said, "Whatever, Mom."

But when the verdict arrived I called her first, wanting to hear the triumph in her voice. She told me that while OJ still stood suspended in disbelief she'd opened the door to her home in Sacramento, stepped out onto the sidewalk and danced a little jig of thanksgiving and joy. She was still breathing hard when she picked up the phone. It was 1995 and I was still young and eager and trying to negotiate the distance between the world from which I'd come and the world in which I lived. Sitting at my desk in the newsroom of *The New York Times,* surrounded by white people pretending hard not to be shocked and pissed at the verdict and its implications, I had to laugh.

There was a time when the image of my mother jitterbugging for a thug and probable-murderer would've made me crazy, and not just because she believed him; half the nation did that. But for my mother, that O.J. thing was deeply personal. She agonized for him, cried for him, prayed. He might've been her child for all the time and energy she spent worrying about him. Decades later she'd spend the same amount of time and energy worrying for Obama, but Obama I could understand. OJ I didn't get at all, so I put it in the closet marked "Crazy Things My Mother Does" and slammed the door.

But that door never stays closed for long. Every few years it pops open, overstuffed and bursting, and I have to dig around inside and rearrange the contents to get the door closed again. For many years this was a frustrating process: it's dark in there, and confusing. I can barely see.

Hers is a strange and knotty mindset, sculpted by racism and abandonment, Southernness and poverty, motherhood and the actions of men both black and white. I know some things about it. I know its strengths: my mother is canny, competent, and smart. I know its foundations: God and family, self-sacrifice and hard work, an appreciation for learning and knowledge and the power they bring. I know its contradictions: she loves Judge Judy and Suze Orman on television but largely distrusts white people in real life. She believes that much of life is misery and is never surprised when things go wrong, but when I call trapped in my own dark chamber she tries to crack open a window with platitudes about things being better "tomorrow," platitudes she doesn't even really believe.

She's come far from whence she began and achieved remarkable things. Not the least of these was raising alone five black children, five children whom nobody expected very much; raising them from poverty to solid and even accomplished lives. But she takes little satisfaction or joy from that accomplishment, a thing which breaks my heart. She believes in God but not in forgiveness.

For Mike Tyson, though, she cried.

I don't understand, and for a long time I held out no hope of understanding nor really wanted to. I am my mother's daughter but our lives have been so different. She is not me.

A couple of months before the OJ verdict I called my mother about some forgettable problem I faced. She told me she'd pray for me, which is her usual reaction. I told her I surely needed it.

"We all need it," she said. "I know my prayers are answered. I know my prayers are answered because I prayed for OJ when they were chasing him. I prayed they wouldn't take his life. I know my prayers are answered because I'm down on my knees every day for Michael Jackson. He needs our prayers."

Me, I live in a world of white atheists and cynical progressives and Cambridge liberals and the idea of praying for OJ or Michael struck me then as both sad and a little off. It seemed, quite frankly, a little crazy.

But given all that my mother has endured, maybe it would be crazy not to be a little nuts.

**

These are the children of Edd and Ella Randolph, my mother's grandparents:

John Edd, Jr., who married Ophelia and begat: Ella Mae, Willie Louise, Ruby, Dorothy, John Edd, Martha Charlene, Leroy, James Albery, Sarah, Annie Mae, Josephine, and Ivory Joe.

Buster, who had no issue.

Dempsey, known as Bill, who married Vera and begat: Jocelyn and Cathlene.

Uncle Elmo who married Pinkie and begat: Elmo, Jr., Melvin, Carol, and Larry.

Bertha, who begat Jimmy, Novella, and Lorraine.

Annie Mae who married Willie Lane and had no issue.

Izola who married Robert Curtiss Lawson and begat: Della Mae, Betty Tuggle, R.C. Lawson, Jr.

Ida Pearl who did not marry and had no issue.

Iola who married three times and begat: Ethelene, Jolene, Jesse, Willie B., Catherine, Randolph, Robert D., Eddie Ricardo, Jacqueline, and Patricia

**

My mother was the oldest of ten children. Her mother, Iola, was the baby of her bunch. These two facts, taken together, say something about the nature of their personalities, and the nature of their relationship.

Iola was a short, sassy, ambitious and good-looking gal they called Baby Rae. She married several times and also didn't marry. Baby Rae moved a lot and left things behind. Baby Rae remains largely an enigma to me. I don't know what she thought or felt about loving men or having their children or leaving both behind. I don't know what she thought or felt about being born poor and black and female in Mississippi in 1919. I don't know what she thought or felt about not getting an education much beyond grade school or working in people's kitchens and bathrooms most of her life or having a daughter who tried to go to college but didn't finish, or having grandchildren who did. I don't know much of anything about Baby Rae because we never spent that much time with her as children and she died before it occurred to me to be curious about such things. It was 1991. I was twenty-seven, just engaged and on my way to Africa for an assignment. She was seventy-two and it was colon cancer.

Colon cancer, by the way, is an epidemic among black folks in general, and black women in particular. It kills us more than anything else. The reasons for this aren't clear to scientists but seem fairly obvious to me. I see them walking down the street every time I drive through the neighborhoods of black Boston: bad diets from poverty and lack of education, low access to health care, the stress of being a black woman in this society—it's all right there at the bus stop, weary and worn and ticking like a bomb. The mothers of two close friends died from colon cancer. My mother had it too, though she survived, thanks to God and her excellent doctors at UC Davis and the common sense to have produced college-educated daughters (including an RN) who both had health insurance and could navigate and advocate her path our nation's byzantine health care system.

What I have of my grandmother is mostly my mother's stories. Here's one: I don't remember when my mother told it to me and I'm not even sure I didn't make it up. It has the ring of truth, though: Baby Rae truth. It involves a dress.

One day my grandmother came home with this dress and handed it to my mother. It was a beautiful, princess dress with tiny roses embroidered on the collar. My mother was so happy with that dress she could've burst; she rarely got nice things. She put that dress on and danced around and the next day she wore it to school and everybody noticed, even the teacher. But when she got home her mother told her to take the dress off.

"But, Momma, why?"

"We have to take it back."

It turned out the salesgirl at the store hadn't checked Ida's credit. But the manager did, and when he found out how bad it was he wanted his merchandise back. So my mother took off the dress and they sponged it out a little and ironed it up and took it back, not telling the man it had been worn.

This kind of thing happened a lot with my grandmother apparently: buying things she could not afford and then having them repossessed. Marrying men she didn't really want, or want long enough or badly enough and then leaving them or having them leave in the end. Same with children.

When I was getting married I asked my mother what I should put on the wedding invitations. Although it is traditional for the mother and the father of the bride to issue the invite I saw no reason to include my father in the deal.

But my mother pushed me to include his name. When I asked why she hemmed and hawed until finally coming out with it. "I want people to know that we were married when you were born."

"Well, of course you were," I said in dismissal and didn't bother to look any further than that. It seemed needlessly old-fashioned, just more of my mother's "stuff," like not wanting to walk me down the aisle or have me walk alone. Eventually we compromised: the invitation read, "Mrs. Ethelene McLarin invites you..."I didn't care, really, and she was content.

Years later my mother said to me, "My father and mother weren't married when I was born. At that time, this was a shameful thing."

I hadn't known until that moment. She'd never told me, and I'd never asked.

**

A few years ago, my mother sent me some sheets of paper in the mail. On the paper she'd typed remembrances of her life. This is some of it:

"Maybe if I write this down I can see how much I can remember of the houses, the people, the fields and the roads that influenced my life.

"He was always there, in my life, my grandfather. I don't remember the first time I saw him. He taught us to spell words at the table. You had to be able to spell *biscuit* or you did not get one. The food itself was not important to me. I liked the feeling of being able to spell words other children missed. He was always there, just like my grandmother, Ella Randolph. I remember more about her than anyone. She would be a great influence in my young days. I remember my grandfather's farm and his farm house as my good place. I was happy there. We didn't starve or go hungry. I remember one time we had nothing in the garden to eat except onions, and Aunt Pinkie fried them and made some biscuits with

12

molasses and butter and we ate many days. We grew most of our food on the farm and usually had fresh vegetables and chickens and hogs and cows and a plenteous supply of food. Even grapes and pecans and walnut trees. Peach trees, plum trees. Everything.

"My grandparents had nine children. Uncle John Ed- dmon whom they called Doc, Aunt Bertha, Aunt Annie, Aunt Izola, Uncle Buster, Aunt Ida Pearl who was called Peg, my mother Iola, whom they called Baby Rae, Uncle Dempsy who was called Bill and Uncle Elmo, the baby boy.

"Uncle Doc was a wonderful person in my eyesight. Every time I saw him I knew we were going somewhere as he was the designated driver for my grandfather. My grandfather had many cars but he never learned to drive. He never had to. Uncle Doc was always there. They were inseparable. Uncle Doc's wife Ophelia was another story. In my lifetime I never heard my grandfather complain about any of his children except Uncle Doc and his wife Ophelia. He just thought it was awful of them to be down there, as he put it, having all those children. Uncle Doc had a lot of nerve having all those children, and he picked the wrong wife and she had nothing and she wasn't even a good worker and she treated Uncle Doc badly, too.

"Yet my grandfather relied completely on Uncle Doc and Aunt

Ophelia, as they were the only ones of his children to not move away and leave him alone. Everyone else moved on as soon as possible, moved up to Memphis and found work other than farm work.

"Aunt Bertha ran away from her home, leaving a husband, a little boy and a little girl. She just up and ran away one day, or so the story was told. She left the two children in the house alone. Someone brought them to my grandparents' house and they raised them. It was years later that the family got in contact with Bertha and by that time she had another family and another little girl.

"When they found Aunt Bertha she moved again, this time to Arkansas, and she raised her little girl in Arkansas. I don't think anyone ever said anything to her about the two children she left. They were raised just like my grandparents' natural children. They were given their mother's share of my grandfather's farm, twenty acres apiece.

"Aunt Annie married Uncle Willie Lane. They never had any children. They moved to Detroit for a while but she moved back to Memphis and after he retired he moved back too. They never got back together but he came to her funeral and wanted to know if he was in her will. He actually said she was still his wife even though he was living with someone and had been living with that lady for many years. The family was astonished.

"Uncle Buster died young.

"Aunt Izola married Uncle Robert Curtis Lawson. They had three children, Della Mae, Betty and R.C. Lawson, Jr. Uncle R.C. went into the Navy and Aunt Izola (Aunt Sis) had a lot of admirers, or so they say. She was small and very well built and very cute, etc. When he came home they got a quiet divorce and the three children were sent to live with my grandparents and their father sent $5 per month for their care. One day little Robert started crying that he was not getting enough food and he was going to tell his father. Everyone begged him to tell, hoping his father would come for him. At that time there were seven children and at least seven adults living in that house and there were only four rooms. Now thinking back I don't know how we did it. My first recollection of my father, Mack Guy, is of me being in his house. It definitely was his house, not my mother's house, not my grandparents' house, and it too was sitting on a small hill. My grandparents lived on this great hill.

"I don't remember how I got to the house. I don't remember who put me in the baby bed. I was young, maybe three years old; this was before my sister was born in 1940. Maybe I slept on the way to their house and they put me in the bed while I was asleep. Anyway they had this baby bed. The bed had high bedrails. I remember crying to get out. The moment is stamped on my mind forever. The picture of me in the baby bed and my dad and his new wife trying to get me to stop crying. I cried harder.

"This is what happened that day. Of course I cannot remember what happened after the baby bed scene as I cannot remember what happened before the baby bed scene. I don't remember the month or the day but I remember that it was evening, not morning and I was thinking I'll cry all night if they don't let me out of this old bed. I did not want to be in their house. I wanted to go home.

"Later on in life I learned more about them. My father and his new wife Lucy, the teacher of our one-room school. She took me to school with her every day. It seems that they wanted to have children and she was unable to conceive. The decision was that they would keep me as I was his own child. My father and mother were not married when I was born."

My grandmother did marry, eventually. After having my mother by one man and another child by another, she married and had four children and then divorced and remarried and produced four more. She was still producing children when my two older sisters were born, which is why I have an aunt one year older than myself (and three years younger than my sister M). One thing country folks can do is reproduce.

The last group of children, the Andersons, got the best of my grandmother's attention. By the time they started arriving my mother had finished high school and was off on her own. She went to Knoxville College, a prodigious accomplishment for people in her family, most of whom had not even completed high school. In the summers she got on a bus with some friends and rode up to Massachusetts or Connecticut to work in the homes of rich white people who had some kind of benefactor connection with the school.

It was while working in Hartford one summer that my mother met my father. It happened at a club where she'd been dragged by her friends. Years later she'd tell us how much she wished she'd stayed home that evening and read.

"Agreeing to go was my fatal mistake," she'd tell us. Sometimes she laughed.

My father was quiet at the club. He seemed as uncomfortable as she, sitting there in the smoky darkness, his crisp Navy whites glowing like the moon. His hair was unprocessed and closely trimmed.

"I'm Benjamin," he told her. "Wanna dance?"

He'd dropped out of school at 17 to join the Navy and this was only the third time in eight years he'd been back home. What went on in their heads? I'm sure the initial attraction was real. My mother as very pretty when she was young, with her stylish, cropped red hair and her cafe-au-lait skin and big, brown eyes. My father was tall and broad-shouldered and striking, especially in his Navy uniform. "Let that be a lesson to you," my mother used to warn us. "Never marry a man in uniform until you first see him out of it. It just might be the clothes."

She thought that because he had traveled the world that he was as ambitious as she and far more sophisticated. She believed they'd explore together, roaming the world and discovering places far beyond the American south or East Coast. But it turned out that what he wanted the most was the life his mother had given his father. He wanted to come back home to Maryland and have by his side someone who'd cook and clean and care for his home while he lived his life. He'd traveled more than enough, as far as he was concerned. He was homesick. When the Navy gave him a choice between bases in Hawaii and Maryland he chose Maryland. Twenty, thirty, even forty

years later my mother remains aghast.

"Can you believe that?" she demands, leaning into my face to see if I will be so stupid as to agree with that man who begat me. "Maryland over Hawaii?"

When the first child came along my father didn't hide his disappointment at my mother's failure to produce an infant male. My mother, who knew who was responsible, was heartsick.

"If he hadn't insisted I would not have had any more children," she told us. "If Michelle had been a boy, none of the rest of you would be here."

But Michelle was a girl and so was Benita and so was I. By the fourth pregnancy my mother was vowing no more regardless. The marriage rose up steadily toward its end.

**

From my mother:

"His new wife was his first wife, or so the story was told to me. In 1937 having a child out of wedlock was a bad thing, not a happy thing at all. It must have been hard on my grandparents. My mother was their baby girl and she was the only one who did not get married before having children.

"My father was very tall. He was at least six-foot- seven. He was very calm, a very calm man. I don't ever remember seeing him lose his temper. My stepmother was small. She cooked small, hard biscuits. The women of that day were noted by their homemaking specialties. One of my aunts was a great pickle-maker; others made wonderful quilts. My grandmother made wonderful soap and good bread. There was always bread on the back of my grandmother's stove. I know because one of my uncles still talks about eating his mother's biscuits. Even the cold ones tasted good. He also says he has never missed a meal in his life, an amazing thing to my mind. I can't remember whether I have!

"I spent the first ten or eleven years of my life on that farm. The road that ran past it was just a country road. I doubt it had a name. I'm sure it had a number as the mailman came down it when the weather was good. If it rained or the weather was bad he stayed on the main road and we had to go two or three miles to get our mail. The road was shaped like a horseshoe. It had houses and farms on both sides. I think the road was a winding property marker. The farms were all big cotton producing farms. It took a lot of land to make enough cotton to live on. Most of the farmers grew everything they needed, except shoes. Tools had to be bought, of course, and some supplies, but it was a great, do-it-yourself time.

"This was Mississippi, the old Mississippi, the one that was not so great at times for black people. It was okay for me as I was a child. It was too much for my father. He left in 1950.

"I remember walking to school with my stepmother. She was our teacher at our little one-room schoolhouse. I remember walking home with her to her house and as young as I was I knew she was not my mother. I also remember that they left me with a family I did not know once. Why I was left there I'll never know. I still remember the front porch of that sitter's house."

As far as I can tell the end of my parent's marriage was the end of Ethelene's life and the beginning of the life of the person I know as my mother. The actual details of the marriage's disintegration are unknown to me, which is probably just as well. I was about four when it happened. I remember: my mother's fat stomach, blood on the carpeted stairway, my mother gone, my pretty Aunt Catherine appearing in the living room, a plane ride to Memphis with M and B and Aunt Catherine, a grandmother I hadn't met, my mother appearing with a new baby brother and sister, a small, one-story, red brick house to now call home.

Growing up I just assumed, because he kept away later when we needed him, that it was my father who'd walked away. Now though I know it was she who left. She believed she had to in order to save us and herself. Strange then, a few years ago, to hear her say, "I wish now I had held onto my family." My sister says she's heard this too. By "family" we both understand she really means "him." After all, she still has us.

The first time I heard this slice of regret it rattled me. My life had been built on the foundational belief that my father wasn't a good guy. Why would she want to go back to that?

My mother returned to Memphis to be near her family and at first things progressed as smoothly as they could have possibly gone. She'd been working at the Post Office in Maryland and within months back in Tennessee she'd landed that most prized of aspiring black possessions for the time: a Good Government Job (GGJ). With a GGJ came decent pay, security, holidays off (or overtime) and a collar on the racism that perpetually threatened to chomp on your neck.

Things worked well for a while. My mother often had to work nights and she'd pay her younger sisters or her maiden Aunt Pearl to stay with us. But as the years passed this got harder; my sister M was a restless teenager and she began to rebel. M was open and pretty and sweet and drew boys to her like a magnet; my mother worried what would happen if she didn't keep her under lock and key.

One night as I stood in the kitchen washing dishes after dinner I heard Aunt Pearl in the living room, her high, piercing voice slicing the house.

"You ain't going nowhere this time of night! Who you think you are?"

"Get out of my way!" warned M. "Get out of my way.

By the time I made it down the hallway and through the dining room they were on the floor, hollering and rolling around. The rest of us stood watching, our mouths agape. To us Aunt Pearl was at least 165 years old.

How in the world could she roll around there on the floor with our sister and not simply shatter, not break into a million bits? But as it turned out, she won. M, probably secretly appalled and ashamed, eventually stopped fighting and stomped off to the bedroom. She didn't go out that night.

Not long after that my mother quit her job at the Post Office. I don't know whether she quit because she was overwhelmed and it was just too much, trying to work full-time and raise five children and protect her budding daughters from the wolves and from themselves. I don't know whether she quit because she was depressed or because her family stopped helping her enough or because some jerk at work was giving her a hard time. My guess: all those things. All I know is that she stopped putting on her uniform in the late afternoon and heading out with a sense of purpose. And that suddenly, things got hard.

We went on food stamps, though not on welfare. My father sent us $200 a month, the court-ordered amount, though my mother always said she got royally screwed by the judge. Even in 1972 $200 wasn't enough for five kids.

Oh, but getting it was exciting. Every day when we were home for summer vacation or something we'd fight to get the mail.

"Mom! The check from Dad!" I'd cry, racing to bring her the precious envelope. It came in the mail, which made it exciting. It came from Him, which made it more so. And $200 seemed like an awesome amount. Faraway, up in the north, my father seemed to lead a rich and glamorous life. He sent us money for our birthdays, but only if we wrote to say what it was we wanted. Occasionally he would stop by during his travels through the state. For a time he was a long distance truck driver. Then he began doing some kind of engineering work for some big company. Once we went to visit him at his home in Pennsylvania. Maybe twice. I don't know.

Did he know how we lived? I don't know. He must have.

We lived hard. When the heat went out we shut off the back bedrooms in the winter and dragged the beds into the dining room. We kept the oven going 24 hours a day to keep warm. And when the hot water heater broke, we heated big pots of water on the stove to take baths.

Thanks to the food stamps, food wasn't really a problem. We never starved, though we ate a lot of cheap, fatty meats and canned mackerel and pasta (we called it "spaghetti," never "pasta") and rice with butter and sugar. Food wasn't a huge problem but cash certainly was. Like everyone, we sold food stamps and at school washed down the humiliating free lunch. For a while my mother was heavy into "couponing," an entire little subculture among the wives and women of

America. I don't mean saving $6.95 at the local supermarket but rather a mini-business of collecting and trading coupons. Boxes of box tops filled our kitchen; we learned never to throw anything out without first clipping the proof of purchase. I'd come home from school and find my mother at the kitchen table with stacks and stacks of box tops and coupons and entry forms laid out in front of her like a royal flush. My mother spent hours addressing envelopes and licking stamps. Getting the mail became an adventure; any envelope could contain a crisp dollar bill or a fifty-cent piece. Some days we collected $15 or $20 or more. Not to mention all the freebies that poured in—free shampoo and cereal, free potato chips and Kool-Aid, free t-shirts and pantyhose and socks. There were years when most of our tee-shirts and almost all of our winter wear came from various manufacturers of boxed or canned goods, which was fine, except this was before wearing the names of food products or other goods on your clothes was cool. I still remember a red ski cap which read "Libbys, Libbys, Libbys" on the front. I hated that cap; all the other kids in school thought it was just the dorkiest thing. Now, of course, it would blend right in.

We also collected bottles and cans and there may have been something with homemade soap at one point or another, I'm not sure. But certainly the most consistent source of income was our paper route.

Every morning before dawn my mother would yell us out of bed,

"Get up!"

"No!" Grabbing the covers and pulling them over our heads.

"Get up, I say!"

"It's dark outside! I want to sleep!"

"You can sleep when you're dead."

Eventually we'd stagger from beneath the sheets and blankets, drag on whatever clothes were required, stumble out to the car. Then it was up our sleeping street and out onto Vollentine Avenue and over to the 7-Eleven parking lot to wait for the paper truck. You had to be there when the truck arrived because someone might snatch your bundles and then you were really screwed. Then it was back to our neighborhood, folding papers and binding them with rubber bands along the way. We all got to be quite expert paper-folders; it's all in the wrist-flick flick.

I hated, hated, hated getting out of bed, but once awake and out into the city throwing papers wasn't really that terrible. There was a kind of muted thrill to being awake when everyone else was still sleeping, to creeping up driveways in the velvety pre-dawn and leaving a paper behind. The real problem was collection day. Once a month we had to go up to those same houses in the middle of a Saturday afternoon and ask for our money. *Knock knock, collecting for the Commercial Appeal, no, don't mind waiting out here in the blazing hot sun and boiling humidity while you scrounge up the change, no, don't mind coming back again six more times before you find that buck twenty-five.*

Worse than the fact that knocking on doors and pocketing pennies made me feel like a beggar on the Calcutta streets was the fact that since this was our own neighborhood, there was always the chance that one of our friends or some kid we knew from school would be opening the door. Delightful. In short, my mother possessed, as many impoverished people do, a certain genius for making impossible ends impossibly meet. Being poor is not easy. Anyone who thinks that it is has never been poor. Being poor costs a helluva lot in time and energy and hopefulness, not to mention cash. Anyone who thinks that all poor people are lazy, and are poor because they are lazy, is an idiot of epidemic proportions. Yes, Mitt Romney: this means you.

Poor people, as a group, are no lazier than anyone else; what they are is disorganized. Disorganized and scattered, adept at putting out the everyday fires that threaten to consume them but hopeless at long-term thinking and making of plans.

This wasn't true of my mother: her long-term plan was to keep us all alive and out of jail and off the street and in school until we were grown. In that she succeeded. This wasn't true of my mother but it was true of many people I grew up with and left behind in Memphis. And the people I interviewed as a journalist and worked with as a volunteer and loved as a distant relative in this my new, middle-class life. Whether these folks can't plan for the future because dealing with the present is so damn hard or whether dealing with the present is so damn hard because they can't plan for the future, it's hard to say. Poverty is grinding. Even long after you believe you've left it all behind.

Here's an example. Last summer my kids and I flew to California to visit my mother, but instead of flying into Sacramento where she lives we flew into Oakland. It's cheaper, only 90 minutes away by rental car (which I have to get anyway) and during the daytime the drive up from the Bay area can be expansive and beautiful. But this time we had a night flight. We were scheduled to arrive around ten but the plane was delayed. By the time we finally landed and got out to the front of the airport to wait for the shuttle bus to the rental car terminal it was after midnight. I opened my phone and dialed the desk of my rental company to tell them we were on our way.

I got a recording: "The rental car counter at Oakland International Airport is now closed. We will open again at 8 a.m."

Holy shit.

I couldn't believe it. My first reaction was outrage: what kind of rinky-dink operation was the Oakland INTERNATIONAL Airport anyway? I looked around; we were the only people waiting at the shuttle bus stop.

Down the way two cabs sat idling at the curb, their drivers leaning against their trucks and chatting in the dim light. Only the occasional car circled otherwise, and behind us the terminal looked dim and deserted. Was the whole frickin airport closing up for the night? Were we going to have to sleep outside on the sidewalk, unsheltered and exposed? I looked over at my children, cranky and tired from the cross-country flight and already bickering.

"Where's the bus?"

"What's taking so long?"

"I'm tired! I want to get to Grandma's house and go to bed!"

Panic. I began working my cell phone but it was hopeless. My mother was too sick to drive down from Sacramento to get us and my brother, the only other family in the area, couldn't be reached. I didn't know anyone else to call, no one to come save us. I called the rental car place at the San Francisco Airport, twenty or so miles and God- knew-how-expensive a cab ride away. Yes, they could rent us a car but, no, not at the same, reasonable internet rate I'd reserved in Oakland. Maybe five times that amount? For a week? Certainly.

By now it was well after midnight and the area was almost completely deserted. I was anxious and scared and the children, picking up on my mounting fear, clustered around. Just as I was about to give in to the panic I glanced cross the highway and saw, glowing in the sky like a sign from above, one word: Hilton.

And as clear as a bell I heard a voice inside my head. "You are not poor anymore. You have a credit card. You can go to a hotel and make your children safe for the night."

I swear to God.

Twenty minutes later my children were sprawled on a hotel bed eating candy bars and trail mix and sipping juice from the vending machine and I was throwing that bolt lock on the door, so high with exhilaration and triumph and relief I could have floated all the way to Sacramento, my children and our luggage on my back.

Back in Boston I told a friend the story. She rolled her eyes. "Well, duh! I would have thought of that first!"

I nodded. She'd never been poor.

When you aren't poor and things go wrong you can sometimes stop them. You can mediate the damage, buy yourself time. You can call AAA and they'll come help you. You can get a second opinion and maybe things will change. You can hire a tutor for your child or take him to a therapist or try another school.

But when you're poor and things begin to go awry, when your plane is late or your car breaks down or your boss hands you a pink slip or you wake one morning and feel a lump, it's only the start of it. When something little or something big goes out of whack it's only the first domino to fall but believe me, the rest are coming. It's the first rock of the avalanche and there's no getting out of the way. So why bother planning what you'll do at the top of the mountain. You probably won't make it there anyway.

So this is what I carry, and I was just a child and thus insulated from the real existential terror of living on the precipice. What more of my mother? What more of her?

**

After my mother lost her job at the post office she slowly withdrew from the world, staying in more often than she went out, turning over more and more of the business of living to us three older girls. First we took over the grocery shopping. It was exciting at first, being set loose in a market and allowed to buy anything we wanted. But then the car broke down and we had to take the bus to the supermarket, which meant lugging everything home that same way. We turned, the three of us, into little mothers- in-training, planning and preparing meals for the week:

fish sticks and French fries, spaghetti and lettuce-and- tomato salad, hot dogs and pork-and-beans.

We'd catch a crosstown bus out of our neighborhood to lessen the chance of running into anyone we knew at the grocery store. Counting out brightly colored food stamps at the cash register was humiliating enough in front of strangers. I always felt the cold eyes of white people boring into the back of my head.

We took over the bill-paying, which meant bus trips to the power company, standing in line. I remember— though, can this be right?—that we even picked up the food stamps. My sisters and I would go alone to the hot, small and crowded office in the strip mall near the hardware store. The line of people stretched past the office door, through the gloomy mall and out into the parking lot. Anyone going into one of the stores in the mall could see you there and know what you were waiting for. They could see you standing in line behind a hundred weary black women, waiting like a dog for whatever leftover bones the world saw fit to toss.

My mother dressed in old skirts and faded housedresses. At first we kids would put our quarters together and for Christmas buy her a new skirt or a nice sweater, thinking that maybe part of the reason she rarely left the house was because she didn't have anything nice to wear. We certainly understood the shame of being underdressed. My mother would "ooh" and "ah" over the skirt, then wrap it back up and put the box on the shelf in her closet. After a while we stopped buying her clothes and bought chocolate-covered cherries instead. She loved those and after she'd eaten all she wanted, we'd get the rest.

My mother wouldn't even go to church, which was fine with me because for a time that meant we didn't have to go either. We just stopped. On Sundays get up and cook fried potatoes and pancakes, then sit around and read the paper (my mother has always taken a paper) or watch Rev. Ike preaching the word on TV. After a few months, though, our Uncle Elmo got wind of us lazing it up on Sunday. Uncle Elmo had his own small, storefront church and was always on the lookout for more members. The following Sundays, my mother got us up and told us to get dressed. But when Uncle Elmo rang the doorbell she just handed us outside and closed the door.

Knowing what I know now, I'd say my mother was clinically depressed. Then again, maybe that's just educated psychobabble; maybe that's just what some people I know would call "white folks' mess." At the time, we just accepted her behavior as being what it was: life. She always washed and combed her hair, even if she never bothered to style it. She was always clean if rarely dressed up. She usually ate after we finished, ate whatever was left over since she had no appetite anyway. She had to put hot sauce on all her food to even taste it. We bought bottles and bottles of the stuff and kept it the pantry. We wanted her to never run out.

**

I am my mother's daughter in many ways, though for years I denied it. I am my mother's daughter: fierce and strong and ready to fight. I am my mother's daughter, intelligent and capable and unwilling to expose the soft part of my belly to nearly anyone. I am my mother's daughter, determined to make for my children a life better than the one I knew and to depend upon no one. I am my mother's daughter, quick to be wounded, long to remember, slow to forgive.

At different points in my life I've tried to explain, dismiss, ignore, romanticize, normalize, and shamefully capitalize upon my mother. As an adolescent, I steered my friends away from our house and made up lies about why my mother rarely came to school. As a scared and floundering black girl at Phillips Exeter Academy, I pretty much kept my mouth shut about my secret, shameful, southern life. As a college student, I told tales of my wacky mother to friends I wanted to like me. Especially white people. Especially white men. I knew it'd seem exotic and profound to them, that I'd seem that way too by extension and maybe they'd love me for that. "This was my childhood," I'd say, launching into one weird story or another. "Hey, if you think that's strange, wait till you hear this!"

Shameful, I know. Mostly garbage anyway: how can I ever really know my mother? How can I even dare to think I could snap together the pieces of that puzzle and make them fit?

Still the impulse remains, especially for a writer. Until we know our mothers how can we possibly know ourselves?

My mother and I had the not-unusual contentious mother-daughter relationship when I was a teenager. We didn't fight as much as my mother and oldest sister, but neither did we get along as well and my second oldest sister and she. As with most things in my life I landed somewhere in-between.

The truth is, she did some things which hurt me. For example: there was the time she tried to bind my feet.

Well, actually she didn't try; she bound them, wrapped them up like sausages for a couple of nights, right before I went to bed. Ace bandages, pulled tight. Hurt like hell. My feet were growing too quickly. I was maybe ten or eleven and they were already ridiculously large. Besides this costing her money she didn't have to buy me new shoes upon new shoes, she said me having big feet would make me unattractive to men when I was older. Men like women with "delicate little hooves." Look at the Japanese. Hey, an idea.

Then there was the time I went with the school honor society, of which I was president, on a trip to New York City. My first trip north, first trip to that amazing city, first big adventure away from home. I saw my first Broadway musical (*A Chorus Line!*) and walked through Times Square and climbed the Empire State Building. I'd never been in a city that large or vibrant. It was a blast. Then we got on the bus and came home and three weeks later my mother burst in on me in the bathroom and demanded to know why I wasn't having my period.

"You're pregnant," she said. Not a question, it was a statement of fact in her mind. Now there was some background here. A year or so before my oldest sister Louise had gotten pregnant at sixteen. This bummed everybody out but especially my mother, who knew personally and bitterly about being a young mother; she'd tried desperately to pass on to us that having children young (or even not so young) and unmarried (or even married) was the surest way for a poor black girl from Memphis to ruin her life. She didn't want to see the same thing happen to the rest of us.

But I wasn't pregnant. There had been plenty of kissing and hickey-making and possibly more on the trip, at the back of the bus and in stolen moments at the hotel, but not by me—in part because no one bothered to ask. I wasn't one of the pretty or popular girls. I was the president of the Honor Society, voted Most Likely To Succeed, soon to be magically plucked from the pack and shipped off to a fancy New England boarding school on a full scholarship. I wasn't a girl boys wanted to kiss. Which I told my mother. Which she didn't believe.

"Why won't you listen to me?" I cried when she kept insisting.

"I don't have to listen to you! I'm the mother!"

For three or four days she monitored my comings and goings in the bathroom and when no blood appeared she dragged me, crying and pleading and furious and humiliated, to the clinic where she bullied the doctor into giving me some kind of pills to "make her period come on." Since this was the 1970s, I have no idea what this mystery chemical might have been: some early version of the morning after pill, perhaps. Whatever it was it gave me horrible, gut-wrenching cramps. For a day or so I lay in bed, devastated and hurting and bewildered by what was happening. Then my period began. After which we went on as before.

A few years later, I was graduating from Phillips Exeter Academy. My mother flew up to New Hampshire, the first time in three years she'd been able to even visit the campus to which her fifteen-year-old daughter had been sent, stumbling, terrified, and alone.

One of the ways I'd survived that experience was by crawling into the world of the theater. I took some acting classes, did a couple of plays, found a fledgling community among the freaks. Starring in a school production of *For Colored Girls Who Have Considered Suicide When The Rainbow Is Enuf,* a production which required the services of nearly every black girl on campus, had been the highlight of my Exeter career, the moment I knew I'd make it, the day I crawled out of the cave and blinked at the light. So theater was important to me, and for graduation I was taking part ("acting" might be too fine a word for it) in a play entitled, as I recall, *Treblinka*—a rough, abstract, experimental thing about the Nazi death camp of the same name. Not exactly *Guys and Dolls*. The play was directed by the chairman of the school's drama department (who'd later be convicted of possessing child pornography, but never mind) and took place on a bare stage with a couple of pieces of scaffolding to represent first the train and later the gas chambers. There was much running around and screaming, much huddling together in terror and flinging ourselves about dramatically. I'm sure from the audience it looked like quite a ridiculous mess but we were serious. We were creating art.

When it was over, all the proud mothers and fathers streamed down toward the stage to gather their progeny in congratulatory hugs. I found my mother at the back of the emptying theater, staring blankly at the floor.

"What's wrong?" I asked her, but she didn't respond.

Before I could ask again the chairman of the drama department came bounding up, flush with triumph and self-congratulation.

"What did you think?" he asked my mother. She looked at neither him nor me but somewhere between the two of us, and gave the little joyless laugh she reserved for white people.

"Did you like it?" the chairman pressed.

My mother remained silent. The chairman looked at me. I looked at the floor.

"Don't you think," the chairman began and finally my mother spoke, cutting him off.

"They've turned my daughter into a fool."

For a long time afterward I thought this painful moment was about me, that my mother was ashamed of the freak I'd become. I could almost see her point.

Here she—this child of poor, black, uneducated Mississippi farm folk—ships her young daughter, her "brightest" child a thousand miles away to a place she's never seen because those people have the secret to winning instead of losing in the world. She takes a risk and three years later she sits in the dark and sees that child shucking and jiving up on the stage. That the white children are right there with her, shucking and jiving too makes no difference; when they climb down they'll still be rich and white.

I could see her point and yet I was devastated and angry and hurt. It was a kick in the gut, which is why I remember it. At the time all I heard were the words *daughter* and *fool.*

Years later I considered that this was really more racial stuff than anything personal. My mother, like any black person born in the Jim Crow south, was profoundly shaped by the confines of racial oppression and so I considered that maybe what this incident really highlighted was the tragedy of racial discrimination on individual lives. Maybe this was just one more example of my mother's issues around white people, around racial stuff. There was a lot of that.

She saw white conspiracies everywhere, but then so do a lot of black people. She thought the plane that blew up over Scotland was the government's fault; they were probably using it to spy on the Iranians or something. Her suspicions of white people lead naturally to feelings of sadness and personal grief for any black man in public trouble. Clarence Thomas, Mike Tyson, James Brown, Richard Pryor: they all received her prayers and passionate support. Michael Jackson. OJ. And so I understood it: how could I expect her not to see the world as *us* and *them* when I myself do so much of the time? Even when I struggle not to. And I was born not in 1937 but in 1964, the year of the Civil Rights Act. And I went to white schools and live in white neighborhoods and married a white man.

But the truth is that black people hurt my mother far more than white people ever did. Racism tangled her in its net, but it didn't fracture her spirit. It was my grandmother's indifference that did that. It was the grinding poverty we suffered because of my father's benign neglect that stuck a stick in that fracture and widened it. It was those, plus a thousand little slights by relatives distant and near—families can be so brutal—and by schoolmates and friends and, I learned very late, one last man whom she wanted to love.

One night a few years back my mother told me a story. When she was 12, her family moved to Memphis from Mississippi. On the first day at her new school, the children teased her mercilessly for being an ignorant country hick (even though Tupelo, Mississippi is not even the toss of a hush puppy away from the Memphis city line). But then the teacher called on her and she stood in class to read aloud and shut them all up.

"People always assumed that they had to be smarter than me," my mother said. "Same thing with your father, who didn't finish high school but who figured that anybody from Mississippi was retarded or something. I got that all the time. I even got it from my sisters and brothers. That's why I tell people, 'You can't hurt me cause I've been hurt by experts.'"

She laughed, a strained and joyless sound that broke my heart. "I've been hurt by people who were supposed to care."

It was then that I decided that the *my-daughter-into-a-fool* incident that had so wounded me was, in fact, about my mother's own woundedness. It was about her own desires. It really had nothing to do with me.

Which also hurt, a little.

This "I've been hurt by experts" talk came just before the cancer journey began. The common depiction of cancer treatment is as a battle: a heroic fight against a tenacious and implacable enemy. But it seems to me more like a peeling. People with cancer are peeled, sliver by sliver, down to their core. What stands revealed is who we are, essentially: faith or fear, optimism or despair, pugnacity or patience or acceptance or rage or love. Or woundedness.

"I'm hurt, I'm hurt." And, God knows, she was. God knows my mother has been hurt by experts.

But here's the thing I think now: so have we all.

For so many I failed to see the wounding, saw only the hardened scabs it produced and I judged and rejected and pushed back against my mother and her hardness and unfathomable views. Then I grew the hell up. Learned about the world she'd crawled out of and the world in which we still lived and I saw, suddenly, the wounds and I was swamped with guilt because I'd contributed; I'd been one of the shackles around her ankle biting into the flesh. So I canonized her as a saint and a hero and all who had hurt her as evil slime and I tried to take some of the pain upon myself, tried badly and without elegance. I invested emotionally in whatever family crisis was underway. I cried a lot after our marathon phone sessions. Then I grew up some more and had children myself and struggles myself and loss of love myself and my own marriage ended and I stood at the crossroads and had to decide which path to take.

Not long ago on the way home from church, I heard a radio interview with a blind seventeen-year-old girl who was at a special chemistry camp. The girl was so grateful to be among other blind people that she just cried and cried and cried. She was trying to decide whether to go back to her regular high school once school began in the fall, or just throw in the towel. She was the only non-sighted person in her old school, and it wore on her: people were forever telling her how brave or inspirational she was or offering other students extra credit to help her or otherwise being idiots. She came into the camp not knowing if she could keep taking it, but left feeling able to go on.

"You can't take all of everything people say to heart because sometimes people don't really mean what they say," the girl said. "Unfortunately, it's just the way the world works."

Sitting in my car I thought, "Amen, sister. Out of the mouths of babes."

The world did terrible things to my mother, the world and its agents: people and life. But here's the thing I've figured out: we've all been hurt by experts. We've all been bashed and pinged and stepped on by all kinds of accomplished bruisers, including that Muhammad Ali of hurting we call Life.

We've all been hurt by experts, and we've all been experts at hurting other folks. And most of the time we weren't even trying. That's the shitty, amazing thing. Anybody over the age of eighteen has already left a trail of wreckage. Some people's trail is like the line of a slug over the morning grass and some people's trail is more like Godzilla through Tokyo, but you know: even the ant the slug crawled over felt the weight on its tiny wee back.

It took me a long time to get this lesson. Some days I still need to start at the front of the book and learn again. I start by looking at my own trail of wreckage. I try to start there.

My own trail has widened and narrowed and at times seemed nearly to disappear, only to explode outward again. I see the skid marks on my ex-husband and my children and some of the guys I've dated and some of my friends and former friends and former students and my siblings and Stella The Wonder Dog and maybe some people at *The New York Times* (I wave to them, unapologetic) and some people I once interviewed or wrote a story about or failed to write a story about. And on God. And on my mother too: my mother is there. To all of you I offer a sincere apology. Except the people at *The New York Times*.

So I can stand at the crossroads and look back on all the rocks which have fallen in my path or been shoved there by other folks and landed on my feet and hurt me. Or I can look at the path of rubble in my own wake and call it square. This I'm trying to do, not only for myself but for my children. It requires a lot of careful stepping and a lot of going slow but I think I'm doing it. I'm doing the best I can.

About twenty years ago while I was still in college, my mother finally escaped the South. I called home one day and found the phone disconnected. It was my sister who told me where she'd gone.

If the moving surprised me, the destination didn't.

During the seventies and early eighties California emanated a kind of siren song for much of my family. One by one the folks on my mother's side of the family all found their way to the Golden State: first Uncle Bill, then my grandmother and her youngest bunch of children. Then my mother and some of hers.

My mother broke from her depression and found a new career: running a group home for mentally disabled children. These children had serious problems—autism, mental retardation, Down's Syndrome. They demanded an enormous amount of time and energy, which she provided without fail. She got them up every morning, bathed and dressed and hugged and fed. Some went off to school or work programs, others stayed with her. She shopped for them, ferried them to the doctor, took them out for ice cream or to the zoo. She washed three or four loads of laundry a day to keep everything spotlessly clean. Like Jerry, these were her kids and she hung onto them with passion. She even adopted one boy who had no one else. Now when I visit I sit beside my "brother" Hector as he stares into the darkness and sings Motown.

It took me no time to see the obvious. By taking care of retarded children my mother created for herself another family, one composed of children who'd never grow up, never cease needing her, never leave behind the incredible sacrifice.

One year my mother sent me a framed photograph of her and the kids, a family portrait from one of those cheesy plastic studios. I chuckled at it. The eyes of children roam all over the place. One girl stares off to the left, two look to the right. Only my mother stares straight ahead.

For this is your home, my friend, do not be driven from it; great men have done great things here, and will again, and we can make America what America must become.

James Baldwin

II:
THE PATTY HEARST OF RACE

I am out walking with my family in our little town, trailing behind with the dog as my husband and children race each other down the street. A smiling white woman approaches my white husband, clipboard in hand. Would he sign a petition for so-and-so? Local boy, running for Congress, out to serve us right. My husband signs. The lady beams. I have heard all this and agree, so up I walk, already reaching for the pen. But the woman jerks her clipboard to her chest.

"Registered voters only, please!"

I am at the park with my children and a friend when a man pulls up in his SUV, opens the door, lets his two dogs out to do what dogs will do. The friend and I, dog- lovers both, cluck our tongues at the inconsiderateness of allowing one's animal to defecate on places where children play. When the man finally hangs up his phone and steps out of his truck to call his animals, my friend and I speak up. To my friend, white, who began the conversation, the man says nothing.

To me he turns and asks, "Do you even live in this town?"

As it happens, I do. My friend does not. The man, who does not, gets into his car.

I am standing near the photo copier when a white colleague saunters up. "Where are you from?" he asks, curious and friendly.

"Memphis."

He shakes his head, unsatisfied. "Where did you go to college?"

"Duke. Why?"

He smiles, relaxed now. "I guess that explains it."

"Explains what?"

"You're the least ethnic black person I know and I couldn't figure out why."

As slights go these three are infinitesimal, scarcely worth remembering. Yet remember them I do. I don't remember what we did after we got home from that walk about the neighborhood, or what I did the morning before the imbecile in the park suggested I was trespassing on the wrong side of town. I don't remember the age I got my period or the name of the kid in the elevator who was in my class last semester or the recipe for sweet potato muffins I have baked a hundred times, but these blips I recall. How my breath caught in my chest. How my heart thudded and my lip curled and my fingers itched. How in the first incident I smiled away my anger while in the second I attacked, lashing the idiot with words even though

I knew my children were watching, their little minds laying down tracks. At the third I just laughed. It was so ridiculous.

Most of all, after each incident I remember thinking, quite clearly: "And that is why I hate white people." Not "That is exactly *what* I hate about *some* white people," which is, possibly, what I really meant. But very specifically, "I hate white people."

I thought those words even though the friend with me in the park was herself white. Also, several close friends, most of my work colleagues and dozens of acquaintances. Also, the man who called me wife.

I lived then, and live now, in what Dr. Martin Luther King, Jr. called the Beloved Community; at least, that's the way it looks. Dr. King's vision was of a completely integrated society, a community of brotherhood and love and justice and easy connection across all spheres of work and social life. From the outside my life probably looks just about right.

My days are filled with close contact with black people and white people, Asians and Latinos, Muslims and Christians and Jews. And white people. A helluva lot of white folks.

I work with white people, I teach their progeny, I live next door and play-group their kiddies and attend their dinner parties and often even sit side by side with them on Sunday morn, during what Dr. King called the most segregated hour of the week. Even the man I lived with until recently, the father of my children, the man I called husband and the man who called me wife, was white. I live about as integrated a life as one could ever dream, or one could ever dread.

And yet the truth is I probably spend more time and energy railing against white foolishness than most of the folks I know who live far more segregated lives. All it takes is some oblivious white chick in the gym reaching out to touch my hair or some repellant Mammy tale penned by a white woman and climbing the bestseller lists to send my blood pressure skyrocketing. *"You is good, Mae Mobley*!" Seriously? Gah.

Shouldn't I, Brown (v Board of Education) Baby that I am, be beyond such aggravation? Shouldn't I know better? Am I preoccupied by race? Certainly some of my friends think so. My white friends want me to drop it because it makes them uncomfortable, my black friends because it seems to them so limited.

To my black friends, white folks and their crazy, pervasive ways are like some malevolent act of nature, like blizzards in Buffalo or tornadoes in Florida: you deal with the nuisance when forced to and forget it the rest of the time. A tornado bears no weight, reflects no light, casts no meaning upon your life unless you allow it to. The great Toni Morrison, speaking of the great Ralph Ellison, asks reasonably, "Invisible to whom?"

In other words, stop defining yourself in relation to white people. When I first read that question from Morrison I flinched. Was that what I was doing? How pitiful.

Whether one envies them as I did in my teens or rages against them as I did in my twenties or disdains them the way I am currently too often wont to do, isn't it much the same? Aren't they still placed at the center of one's life? The opposite of love is not hate, it is indifference. I crave indifference. I'm getting there now, steadily and surely. But for many years I was closer to hate.

Oh, I know: I'm a racist. That's the easy out. Some people, smug and secure in their privileged, insulated, easy-living-liberal worlds will be appalled by such sentiments and write me off. Many of these people have already left the room, on their way back to Cambridge, no doubt. Folks, please drive safe.

James Baldwin said: "Nobody is more dangerous than he who imagines himself pure in heart, for his purity, by definition, is unassailable."

In Barack Obama's post-racial America the only racists left are black people and cartoonish movie buffoons. Nobody in the Tea Party is racist, for example, not even those who refer to the president as a tar baby or send out emails of the first family depicted as chimps. Nobody in the far right chattering class is a race-baiting ass; certainly not Glenn Beck or Rush Limbaugh or insert-name- here. The good Lord knows none of those birther lunatics running around demanding the president show his papers have a racist hair in their nose. And if these good folks have somehow resisted internalizing three hundred years of racial hegemony, if these proud and decent citizens can look themselves in the mirror each morning and raise their hands to swear they are pure and free from bias of any kind, then who the hell cannot? Except black people.

Got it? All racist thinking and racial disparities in American society and American hearts, in housing and education and juvenile justice and banking and love and everything else, got dissolved with Martin Luther King and washed down the drain by Oprah.

We're clear. We're good to go.

But the interesting question is not why I once felt the way I did. The interesting question feeling the way I did, I continued to five the life I lived?

Why would a person make her life among people who set her teeth on edge? If trapped was what I felt, why didn't I just escape?

Was this Stockholm Syndrome, my life? Am I the Patty Hearst of race?

··

In many ways I was born to integrate. I arrived a Southern, black child in the late spring of 1964. It was the eve of Freedom Summer, one month before Cheney, Goodman and Schwerner took their fateful journey in Mississippi, two months before President Johnson signed the Civil Rights Act into law, ten full years after Brown.

When my parents separated my mother moved from Baltimore, Maryland back to her second hometown of Memphis, Tennessee. Her first hometown, the place she was born, was Olive Branch, Mississippi, but most people she knew had already clawed their way out of that desolate backwater and none were going back. Memphis, though retrenchment, was not so terrible: the South, but the Mid-South and not the Deep, a city of aspiration and some reasonable size. She arrived some four months after Martin Luther King was killed. My sisters were eight and five, the twins were newborn. I was four years old.

Ten years earlier, in 1958, the parents of little Gerald Young, aged eight, had tried and failed to enroll him at all-white Vollentine Elementary School, a few blocks from my house. But in 1960 a federal lawsuit was filed and by the time we showed up my mother was able to get her children through those same Vollentine doors with scarcely a word. Maybe nobody brought out the lemonade but nor did anyone stand glaring in the doorway, hearts and arms crossed. Nobody called us names or unleashed the dogs. Nobody threw rocks at the car.

From kindergarten on I sat in the classroom with children both white and black and thought little of it - the sitting together, I mean, not the racial differences.

We weren't that advanced. Some people were black and some people were white (in Memphis, that pretty much summed it up, or so we thought) and that distinction meant something important—all this was glaringly apparent to everyone. But not enough to keep us apart. My two best friends in elementary school were black girls, which grew out of similarities, but I was friends with many white children in my class. Betsy and I walked home together, though she stopped at a nicer house. Denise and I practiced our songs for the school talent show on the sidewalk outside her house, though she never invited me inside. Our worlds were neither completely separate nor of a piece, but for the most part, we all just got along.

It was a golden age of integration, sweet but brief. In 1970-71, the year I entered first grade, enrollment in the Memphis public schools reached a high of 148,000. In 1973, third grade for me, the city implemented a court ordered, full-fledged desegregation plan that included busing as a remedy. White reaction was calm. By the time I reached fifth grade more than 30,000 white students had fled the public schools, and the numbers would keep on tumbling. Today the Memphis system, like most urban districts north and south, is nearly 90 percent "children of color." In Memphis, for the most part, children of color means black. Segregation to re-segregation in forty years flat.

But when I was a child, at least as far as school was concerned, white people were always in the mix. White students, white teachers, sometimes white principals. I had some vague idea that it had once been otherwise, but nobody really spoke of it.

**

A few years ago, at work, I took part in a racial dialogue group: fifteen of us, black, white and Latino, trapped together in an overly-air conditioned room with weak coffee and a bright-eyed facilitator beaming out love. After all the white folks in the room had been assured of their safety and the black folks duly warned, we moved on to our first exercise: filling in bubble diagrams with words we might use to describe ourselves: mother, scholar, Christian, Bostonian, etc. We were told to make sure to reserve one bubble for race or ethnicity.

We were then told to star the word which most described who we were, and then we went around and said which attribute we'd picked and why. Some of the white people were surprised that all of the black people picked race and I tried to be surprised at their surprise but I couldn't pull it off. One white woman did pick white as her most salient attribute and one black man expressed surprise but then she said she'd been through diversity dialogues before and so in the end that wasn't really a surprise either.

In the second exercise we were asked to imagine we were hosting a party that weekend. What kinds of people, racially and ethnically, would be likely to attend? The black folks all had rainbow guest lists. The white folks were all partying among themselves. Surprise.

One woman voiced defiance: "Well, of course they would all be like me. They'd be my family, my friends and neighbors. That's the world I grew up in."

Most of the other whites, though, climbed dutifully aboard the train of guilt and headed off for an hour or so in self-recrimination land. "When I was in college I had friends of all stripes," said one professor. "Now my life, I admit, is homogeneous. What happened, I wonder?"

He sounded genuinely bemused. All around the table people shook their heads in sad commiseration, as if racial isolation was something that snuck up on a person and caught them unawares, like a televised presidential address, or avian flu.

But of course the truth, for this man, as for many of the good, right-thinking whites I know, was that racial integration is utterly superfluous to a good and right thinking kind of life. A bonus if you had it, not to worry if you did not; not even icing but candy sprinkles on the cake. No decisions were based upon it, at least not conscious ones, and so the town he lived in was chosen for its schools and the schools for their "quality" and the neighborhood for its "historical beauty" and the church for its "sense of community."

And once a year he gets to be shocked, shocked! to find his life so utterly segregated. So unrelentingly white.

**

I was in sixth grade the first time I heard the word Oreo directed not at a cookie but at myself. Sixth grade, in our primary education system, is the critical juncture by which we've all been sorted into what Jeff Howard of the Efficacy Institute describes as one of the three groups into which we are taught to believe all humans fall, intelligence-wise: very smart, kinda smart and kinda dumb. I'd been tagged as very smart, which meant I took classes that were kinda hard, like algebra or chemistry, instead of kinda easy. Or just plain pitiful.

It also meant that, since elementary school, myself and maybe twenty or twenty-five of the 180 or so kids in my grade level were pulled out of class for an hour or so each day for "enrichment." The program was called CLUE, for Creative Learning in a Unique Environment and we did things like build working models of the solar system and take field trips to the science museum and write, direct and stage our own three-act plays while those left behind in the regular classroom, clueless and un-enriched, recited the pledge and practiced handwriting and learned how to make change. At first those left behind focused only on the egghead element, teasing and torturing us Cluers as a group for being too damn smart, but by sixth grade things had shifted. By sixth grade, the blinders were off and even the clueless noticed a certain racial discrepancy in who got enriched and who did not. Naturally, they took out their anger and frustration not on the teachers and principals who perpetuated this inequity, or on the whites kids, dwindling in percentage of school population by the year, but on us, the handful of Very Smart black schnooks. "Oreo," they sneered as I passed in the hallway. "Black on the outside, white on the inside," they hissed. "Think you so smart, talking all proper and everything. You must think you a white girl!"

Which stunned me, really.

Because who had even considered such a ridiculous thing? I was black, my family was black, my life was what it was. I ate greens and corn bread and banana pudding. I went to church on Sunday and watched Soul Train on Saturday afternoons. I loved the Jackson Five and the Commodores and Rufus featuring Chaka Kahn (also Barry Manilow but no one but my sisters knew that awful truth).

Also I was stunned because by sixth grade every female child has sorted herself into one of three groups into which we have been taught to believe all females of the species fall, lookswise: very pretty, kinda pretty, ugly as sin. I was ugly as sin, or so I thought. And this ugliness had much to do with the fact that my hips were big and my nose broad and my skin dark and my hair kinky and short—in other words, that I was about as far from being white as Olivia Newton-John was from being anywhere close to cool. I wasn't stupid. I watched television. I watched *a lot* of television and like everybody else I understood that Charlie's Angels were the standard against which we were all to be judged.

But none of that mattered in junior high.

Harvard economist Roland Fryer has found that black students do indeed pay a price in popularity for academic success, but only certain ones. Black students at private schools and black students at predominantly-black public schools can get good grades without sacrificing friends, but black students in integrated schools see a notable dip in popularity for every letter grade they climb. My black classmates, struggling against the systematic non-enrichment of their lives, pinpointed me as enemy. And so my alienation from my own people began.

Toni Morrison says that whenever she slammed up against some example of racism or naked white contempt her father would tell her, "You don't live in that neighborhood." You don't live, in other words, in their imagination of you. That's not your home. And so she was not scathed.

But what if it happens in your own neighborhood? What if you become suddenly unwelcome in your own home?

**

When I was fifteen a white man showed up at my school in Memphis talking about a special kind of high school, one that boarded students like thoroughbred horses and trained them well and sent them galloping onward to conquer the world. A group of us very smart kids were sent to the auditorium to hear his lecture and watch his slides and be sent home with his glossy application brochures. I tossed mine on the kitchen table, having no interest in going to a school (Phillips Exeter Academy) I'd never heard of in a state (New Hampshire) I couldn't pick out on the map. But my mother had other ideas.

Ten months later I walked off a plane at Logan Airport and, following directions that had been sent to me in the mail, found my way outside to a waiting bus. I don't remember much about this trip; I don't, for example, remember whether I spoke to any other students on the hour-long drive up to New Hampshire; possibly I was in shock and so did not.

The school had assigned one of the older black boys, a returning senior named Kevin, to meet me at the bus and walk me to my new dorm. Like every other black girl on campus, I would grow to love Kevin; he was tall and elegant and confident and hopelessly faithful to a mysterious girl named April who had graduated the year before. I think the school sent Kevin along that first, hazy-dazy, bewildering day to give me some visual grounding point, some point of reference to assure me that I had not, in fact, left behind the recognizable world. Kevin left me at my dorm, and I walked upstairs and into my room and met the girl, sun-blonde, bubbly, oozing her father's love, who would be my roommate. Later that week I met the boy who would become my first boyfriend. His name was Geoff and he was white but he was the blackest white boy I have ever known. He was, in fact, blacker than I was, if being black meant speaking slang and knowing about the Sugar Hill Gang and growing up in Spanish Harlem and having a black man (his stepfather) around the house. He thought it did. I thought him wonderful.

Possibly this is where the confusion began.

Oh, but at Exeter I was blacker than I had ever been at Snowden Junior High. None of the forty or fifty black students on campus (out of an enrollment of approximately 1000) ever questioned my fitness as a member of the race; I was welcomed with grasping, open arms. I joined the Afro-Exonian society, I puppy-tailed the black upperclasswomen, I even joined, briefly, the cheerleading squad. Yes, cheerleading. It was an all black squad, non-competitive and generally looked down upon as being un-academic and un-cool. All of which should have made it a perfect fit. Except I just couldn't swing those little pleated maroon skirts. I felt ridiculous.

Those black upperclasswomen were my lifeline that first year, the only thing which kept me hanging on. Especially after Geoff dumped me, which devastated me, just broke my little heart. And when he started dating a white girl shortly after that I thought I would just curl up in a fuzzy brown ball and roll away. Then he got kicked out of school for something or the other. So that helped.

By senior year, when all the black upperclasswomen who had sheltered me were gone and I was alone and yearning and my butt and thighs seemed unnaturally huge and I was tired of explaining about my hair and of representing the black point of view in class, and I'd been called nigger while walking the streets of the town more than once, and I had fallen in and out of love with a bushel full of boys black, white and Asian but none of them with me—by then I was pretty much a mess: cynical and self-loathing and confused and pissed. Angie Davis lite. A freak back home in Memphis. A curiosity in the great, white North. What, exactly, had that place turned me into? What exactly was I anyway? At Exeter I came to mourn myself as black, and to distrust and dislike white people as white. On the positive side, I got a good education (though not nearly so grand as they supposed) and found the writer in myself.

So I guess it all evens out in the end. Right?

**

Years back I donated copies of two of my novels to an auction, along with an offer to speak to the book club or gathering of the bidders choice. When the winning bidder contacted me to set a date, she asked which of the two novels her book club should read. I strongly suggested the second, which is about interracial relationships, rather than the first, which is about racial anger, not because I don't like my first book but because I was trying to make life easier on myself. The bidder was white and I knew all the members of her book club would be as well. I didn't want to have to sit in a living room full of white chicks and explain why the first thing the character in my first novel does is slap her white colleague across the face.

But of course they read the first book anyway. And of course it was an excruciatingly awkward conversation, full of fits and pauses and speaking in different languages. Two of the women in the group said not a word the entire hour I was present, just picked at their food and glanced nervously out the window, as if searching for their husbands to come and rescue them. Another woman simply insisted the character's righteous but self-destructive anger had nothing to do with race. When I told her she was wrong and that I was pretty sure I had the inside track on my character's motivation she brushed me aside.

"No," she insisted. "That's not it. It's got to be something else."

The evening made for an interesting contrast with one I'd had six months before, this one speaking to a black book group which had read the second book. The woman who'd invited me to this club, a smart young sister with beautiful locs, a member of my church, a woman with whom I'd hoped to be friends, launched the night with a declaration:

"When I see a black woman walking down the street with a white man I assume she has no racial pride."

Um, awkward. Awkward moment. But not one for which, after twenty years with a white man, I was completely unprepared.

This question of racial pride is one any thinking person involved in a relationship with a white person had damn well better ask herself. That it is not a question the white person involved has to ask is irrelevant; the black person had better ask because she needs to know the answer. She needs to know because there's a busload of people coming around the corner clutching their own two cents, clutching their own garbage or venom or fuzzy, suffocating clichés, and they're ready to hurl all that mess right on top of your relationship and you better have a shovel to dig it out. For every cry of *jungle fever* comes the answering call that *love is colorblind!* But the thinking black person neither bows to the one nor rests on the other. The thinking black person stops and asks because the legacy of slavery and oppression is the legacy of self hatred and there is no denying this truth. Malcolm X understood this. Martin understood it too, but his solution to the problem was too elevated, too enlightened for the great, mean mass of us. Martin wanted us to love white people, to love our enemies, to see the worst Bull Conner as ourselves, sinners in need of salvation. Malcolm said, "Screw that!" We didn't need to love white people. We needed to love ourselves.

Because we didn't. Malcolm saw that, saw it plain as day. Malcolm knew that black self-hatred was one of the most intentional and crushing inheritances of slavery and he knew we had to get over it. I'm saddened to report we have not gotten over it yet.

I take my daughter to a black barber shop to get her hair chopped off because she's four and doesn't care and my life needs simplifying, but not one not two but three stylists just flat-out refuse the dirty deed. "Are you crazy, girl? This child's got *good* hair! If it was nappy that would be one thing but don't you even think of cutting off all that pretty, pretty good hair."

And that, really, is just the tip of the iceberg.

**

I'll admit it: I cried on election night 2008. When the newscasters announced that Barack Obama had won the race for the presidency of the United States I fell on my knees and let the tears run down my face. My daughter came up and hugged me. My son patted me on the back.

I cried not because I believed racism or racial inequities had suddenly died in America and that we would all join hands and walk happily into the sun, but because I was one of those people who never thought she'd live to see even that day. The scholar and writer Randall

Kennedy says people who believed as much aren't saying much for their fellow citizens, and this true: I was not. I did not believe the great majority of my fellow Americans were ready to elect a black man to lead them, regardless of his talents or abilities. Best girlfriend, yes; president, no. I didn't think I'd see it and I'm not sure I'll see it again. Given what's happened, I'm not sure I want to. That poor man has been treated like crap.

I predicted as much. I wrote an essay for an online magazine in July of 2008 in which I suggested that the worse things looked for the average American at the time—and they looked bad—the better the chance that Obama would win the presidency. Not because Americans were sick to death of George W. Bush or because we'd finally had enough of Republican policies that enriched the rich, endangered the poor and alienated us from the world community (sigh). No, I predicted Obama would win because America was in the waning days of its glory, and black folks always get the tail end of things.

Freshman year, Duke University I decline to join a black sorority and am immediately tagged by my black dorm floor-mates as insufficiently black. That I also decline to join a white sorority (not caring for sororities in general) holds no water in the matter: I am a sellout, a white girl wannabe, an Oreo. My mother, who had high hopes for me becoming either a Delta, or, if the winds of luck were really at my back and the lighting in the room was sufficiently dim, an AKA, puts down my refusal to even consider the idea as just more proof that too much exposure to white people has left me confused.

Instead I find my own ragtag group of friends, many of them, though not all, white. I don't know why this is, and I don't want to think about it much; I'm struggling just to keep the head above water. I go to class. I work as much as possible to keep afloat as the financial aid diminishes. I develop a strong crush on a tall, good-looking and startlingly intelligent football player, black, who is sweet but treats me like a younger sister. Not a single black man on campus so much as looks my way. A few white guys do, so I go out with them or have fitful, awkward sexual encounters. Eventually I meet M, a very kind white suburban boy trying to figure out his own life. M will become my husband. The years pass, my racial complication and resentment simmer and stew.

Then out into the working world. In Greensboro, North Carolina I become the first black reporter for the local newspaper ever to cover the city council, a distinction so pathetically dubious I am, at the time, surprised anyone thinks to point it out. But they do. Repeatedly. One of the city council members, an astonishingly dippy white woman, tries to set me up with the one other black person she knows, her mailman. I decline.

After a couple of years I receive a job offer from *The Philadelphia Inquirer.* I accept, leaving M temporarily behind as he finishes his degree. In Philadelphia I take self defense classes, because this is the first big city I've ever lived in, and then walk the streets of North Philly hunting "positive stories about the community" that nobody ever reads.

But, lo and behold, something strange and important happens. There is, among the handful of black reporters on staff, a kind of family. And they take me in.

Terry is young and ambitious and funny, a Trini charmer from New York. Larry is calm and thoughtful and courtly, a Southern gentleman. Vanessa is Vanessa, a tall, gorgeous fashion force unto herself. Somehow we all fall in together, more or less. We call ourselves BORM: Black Organization of Reporters on Metro or something like that, and email one another during the day and head to lunch when things get hard and for drinks after work to bitch and commiserate. It makes our white colleagues nervous to see us going to lunch en masse, which of course means we want to do it more. *Don't smile when you walk past Fred. Just glance back at me and give a black power salute.*

Slowly, slowly I realize what I've been missing, why the wind was whistling through. I lived in Germantown, on a quiet little block of tidy row homes inhabited by families black and white. I'd found a church, an interracial United Methodist congregation just up on the street. I had a boyfriend who was white but tried to understand.

On the surface I was living an integrated life, but what that really meant was a white life with a little black mixed in. My neighbors all got along but did not really socialize. The interracial church was really a white one, progressive and open-hearted, but white in its heart and at its core. The few black folks wedged in did not change the wood.

But talking smack with the gang over lunch at the Vietnamese place or drinking wine and playing cards at Vanessa's on a Saturday night felt like home in a way I had not felt since my first year at Exeter, when those older girls reached out and pulled me in from the waves. Or really, since leaving Memphis. Memphis with all its trouble and heartache and pain, but home nonetheless. Home is where they have to take you in, even when they'd rather not. In Philadelphia I found my way back home and I realized how much I needed to be there.

After Philly I would never again move to a new city and not seek out some form of structured black community.

The Nineties begin: Marion Barry and Washington, D.C. Nelson Mandela and the ANC. George Bush and Rodney King. The L.A. riots and welfare queens. Bill Clinton and Lani Guinier. I marry my husband.

We buy a house in the Germantown neighborhood, on a block overflowing with integrated pride and within months comes the call from New York. I turn it down at first but eventually I relent and join the staff of the *New York Times.* The Great, Gray Lady. I am swept aboard with a great wave of other eager, bright young colored folks in a storm of enthusiasm and good intentions all around.

Sweeping past us toward the door are the previous wave of bright and talented colored folks, embittered, exhausted, but never mind. Management smiles, all good intentions and bafflement. We put down our heads and work. I put my head down and work and when I stumble into a corner and ask for help people say, "Go ask your rabbi. Who's your rabbi?" and I just laugh because I have no idea what they mean. Later, when I finally figure it out, I stop laughing. "Nobody," I say. The man who would presumably hold that title, the man who has brought me inside, is a man named Gerald Boyd, the only black man among a slew of assistant managing editors and later the first black managing editor itself. But Boyd does not covet the position. "Don't want to be the black folks' editor," he tells me and others, in so many words. It is a decision we all despise and completely understand. Years later Boyd would find himself unfairly wrapped up in the wrinkled mess of the liar Jason Blair and unceremoniously tossed into the trash.

The Nineties pass.

Looking back, what amazes me most about those two decades, the 80s and 90s, of my life was how furious I was for so much of them, how aware of the fury and yet helpless to end it nonetheless. At one point while I was working at the Inky things got so bad I went to therapy. The first therapist, plucked from the phone book, is white, blonde, leggy and smart and sympathetic; I hate her on sight. The second one is also white, frizzy-haired and grandmotherly; she sits in a rocking chair and nods soberly while I sob. The third, who I secure after much hunting, is a super-dignified black woman in whom I place great hopes. During our first session she sits with her mouth slightly twisted and listens to my confusion with such icy remove I feel slammed right back into junior high.

Each time, after a few, cathartic sessions of abundant tissue use, I begin wondering what, exactly, these paid pity parties are supposed to accomplish? Self-knowledge? But I already knew my stuff, only too well. I knew my anger was outsized. I knew my anger was damaging no one but myself. But still I could not let it go.

One therapist, the grandmother, beams as I run down my list of issues: absent father, damaged mother, immersed in whiteness and cut off from black. "Your self-analysis is dead-on," she coos. "You're very impressive!"

At the time I just wept a little and wrote her out a check, but looking back I see the irony: instead of helping me address the core issues of my life, this woman and the others of her kind had merely replicated them. The together blonde. The disdainful, judgmental sister. The grandmother who wanted to help me **get over** my feelings about race instead of moving through them. *You're very impressive*, the grandmother beamed.

If I had a dollar for every white person who's ever said those words to me I'd give my pocket change to Bill Gates. Some days I think I should hang a shingle on my forehead: *Impressing White People Since 1964.*

But it also while at the *Inky* that I make my first trip to Africa. The Motherland.

"How'd you like to go to Liberia?" asks my editor.

"Sure!" I cry, the eager cub. "Sign me up!"Then I scurry back to my desk and try to figure out where the hell is this place called Liberia.

Turns out it's on the west coast of Africa. Turns out it was founded in 1847 by a bunch of formerly enslaved or born-free-but-barely African Americans and their white benefactors. Most of whom wanted them safely removed from "mixture" and had visions of shipping every last black folk in the land "back home."Turns out those black people, escaping slavery and vicious racism and exclusion from the full rights of citizenship in the country of their birth, went to Africa and proceeded to establish a new nation that looked almost freakishly like the old.

"Visiting Liberia for the first time," I wrote in my first dispatch from the motherland, "is like stumbling across a little sister you did not know you had."

It wasn't just the flag (red, white and blue, with one star instead of fifty) or the governing structure (a declaration of independence, a constitution, three co-equal branches of government, sound familiar?) or the capital city (Monrovia, named after U.S. president James Monroe) or the surnames of the long-ruling political and business elites called Americo-Liberians (Tubman, Johnson, etc.) What looked most familiar was what had happened when those first fleeing black folks stepped off the boat onto the fertile, lush shores of Africa and looked around. "Nice place."

"Yeah."

"Let's take it!"

"Cool! But, um, what about the folks already living here?"

"No problem. We need somebody to relegate to the bottom layer of society, while we dominate the business and economic rungs and get rich."

Yeah, okay: a snarky oversimplification of the long and complicated history of Liberia. But not much. And if, if, I'd ever actually held the simplistic, reductivist view that white people had done such terrible things to black people because white people were evil plain and pure, well, then, Liberia took care of that. Not about white and black. Not evil and good, devils and the long suffering saved. It's about power and opportunity, clear and true.

Them that's got shall get and keep on getting, as long as they possibly can. Humans will do what humans will do.

Still, that universal truth does not diminish the more particular truth of American history. Or its very real and present legacy.

What might begin to diminish such truth, or at least transform it, would be the clear, undefended acknowledgement of the whole long history and present implications of whiteness and lingering white privilege by the majority of white Americans. This is what I figured out, finally: it's not white people I hate but whiteness and white privilege. This may seem a hairsplitting conclusion but it is not. It's a critical distinction, one that allows me to live with the cognitive dissonance that is my life. It is, in a fashion, the distinction at which Malcolm arrived during his pilgrimage to Mecca, the one that set him free from hatred but not from history. It's a distinction that allows a fact-finding but not a faultfinding. It's a distinction that can save your life.

**

And so on and so on, into marriage and motherhood, out from daily journalism and into writing and teaching, out from one cold, white northeastern city and into the next and then the next. And so on and so on and scooby dooby doo-bee. We got to live together, or maybe we don't.

These days I still live a far more integrated life than probably most of America. Some of my best friends really are white, but just a few. What, I wonder, separates them from the dozens upon dozens of more distanced white acquaintances with whom I will never share a sincere and honest conversation? Maybe it's that most of my real white friends have lived some experience that offsets their privilege: some childhood trauma or major absence, some addiction or tragedy, some societal setting apart. Those who have not have simply, out of some bewildering sense of interest, sat down to unpack the knapsack of whiteness and to examine the privilege that goes along. Thus we are able to connect.

When we talk about race, these friends and I, I am careful to distinguish the behavior from the skin color. I do not indict or generalize, they do not apologize or defend. I don't have to care-take their feelings of collective guilt or accusation. They don't have to care-take mine of collective victimization or denigration. We. Just. Talk.

These friends are few.

The truth is, most of the time I'd just as soon hang out with my black friends, and not least because it's simply easier. Or maybe I'm just weary of trying to live a truly integrated life when so many others have abandoned the project. When the nation itself has given up.

In the end Patty Hearst was pardoned for her crimes. But when do the rest of us get off?

III:
DIVORCE DOG

The trick is to love somebody.... If you love one person, you see everybody else differently.

James Baldwin

My dog Stella follows me everywhere. Down to the kitchen for a cup of coffee, upstairs to the room where I write, downstairs again when I need more cream.

"Stop," I tell her. "Back off, please. You're suffocating me. Have your own life. Have some dignity."

She listens not, just follows me into the bathroom for my shower, nosing open the door I try to close in her face. One minute I'm standing there daydreaming beneath the water, lost in my lavender-scented dreams. The next minute I am startled awake by a pair of lipid brown eyes gazing up through the spray. Such undemanding, unrelenting, unconditional love. It makes me furious.

"Go away, Divorce Dog," I mumble, tripping over her as she sprawls beneath my feet on the kitchen floor. It's six o'clock and I'm rushing to make dinner for my children. Were it just me I'd have a bowl of cereal and be done with it. Cooking bores me to tears; food is fuel as far as I'm concerned. Except for French fries. I love French fries. But you can't serve a diet of French fries and baby carrots to your children. They'll gain a few pounds in their ugly duckling stage and the pediatrician will hound you like a criminal.

Instead you must calculate each meal as carefully as a scientist: this much protein (though you really should become a vegetarian) and this many fruits and vegetables (you aren't giving enough or enough variety) and this much starch (so what if the kids want more? Pasta is poison! White flour is like cyanide! Refined sugar is worse than heroin!).

But this is a first-world problem, how much food to cook; to even complain is indulgent and self-absorbed. Guilt upon guilt.

I take it out on the dog, who lies directly in the path between oven and sink.

"Get out of here!" I scream. Under my breath I add, "Damn divorce dog!"

Under my breath because the children are home: one in the living room watching television, the other in the dining room rotting her brain on the internet. I do not refer to Stella as Double-D in their presence. They probably sense she's a divorce dog but we do not speak of it.

**

I wouldn't say I was a dog person.

I wouldn't say, in fact, that I was an animal person, in general. I mean, I like animals well enough. I think horses are awesome and dolphins are slick and I spend the extra two dollars to buy eggs from hens which have been allowed to live free on the range. I like to watch those PBS specials on the impressiveness and intelligence of *working* dogs: dogs that help the blind or track the lost or detect epileptic attacks before they take place.

But I am not, in general, sentimental about animals. Stella is not like a child to me. When the lovely young trainer at the MSPCA dog obedience class kept referring to me as Stella's mommy I had to gently object. Only two beings in this world can consider me "mommy," I told her, and both of them possess the ability to sweat.

I would not pay hundreds of dollars for an animal (I consider the shelter adoption fee a donation toward their good work and also a reasonable price for making sure my house is not overrun by little Stellas, not the cost of the dog). Every time the vet tries to guilt me into anything more than the basic rabies-heartworm cocktail I just hold up my hand. I find astonishing the fact that Americans spend $50 billion a year on our pets, which is like a gazillion dollars more than the GNP of 64 countries, and about six times what we spend grudgingly on Head Start.

To each his own, of course. But seriously, come on.

Moreover, if pressed to take a side in age-old domestic animal divide I'd probably have to side with the cats. Cats, I can relate to. Cats are solitary and aloof and, let's face it, are largely disdainful of us. Cats are observers; they're watching you, whether you know it or not. They're paying attention. They're keeping score.

That I would be, technically, a cat person who ends up owning several dogs might *seem* contradictory, might even *be* that way. Except that contradiction has been the standard of my life. Looking back over the five decades of my time on this crumbling, heating earth I see my days
laid out in a series of yin-yang opposites struggling not to spin apart:

There's the Southern girl who got stuck in the North. The child of welfare who has mingled with the rich and powerful. The proud and sometimes angry black woman who married a white man. The anti-social journalist. The unbelieving Christian. The mother who loves her children but not motherhood.

Probably the only part of my life which has never faced internal contradiction is my writing. The world of my work, which is the world of my creation, is the only one in which I've never been pushed to choose sides. Which is probably why writing has saved my life.

So, put into that context, the fact that I'd end up with this dog following me around and driving me batty makes perfect sense. Clearly, I am supposed to learn something from this animal. Clearly she's supposed to teach me something deep and meaningful about life and loyalty and love—at least, that's what all the bestsellers say. But what, precisely, I'm supposed to learn from a being who spends half her time licking her nether parts and the other half mauling the vacuum cleaner is unclear to me.

**

When M and I first met he lived in a cluttered apartment in Durham, North Carolina with a bunch of really smart, slightly helpless and mostly-stoned other guys and a really smart, utterly competent and mostly-stoned (on catnip) cat named Motorhead. I was twenty years old, finishing up my sophomore year at Duke University and racing as hard and fast as I could away from my childhood and toward a better life. M was twenty-one and a little stalled. He was also white and I was black but that didn't particularly bother me; I knew a lot about white people, having had to learn. Cats, on the other hand, we unknown to me.

We'd had a couple of dogs when I was growing up in Memphis. Mr. Carter and Weepie were their names and they lived their lives either outside or in the mudroom on the side of our house. My mother, like many Southern black people, did believe animals actually belonged in the house and she certainly did not believe in cats. Cats were devious and possibly evil. They sucked the breath from babies. They trafficked in witchcraft. That sort of thing.

Motorhead was probably the first cat I ever knew. He was awesome, a fat, lazy gray tabby with diamond eyes and Southern charm. Maybe it was all that catnip but he was never aloof. He would greet me the minute I stepped into that grubby male palace and if I sat on the couch for any length of time he would come and sleep on my lap, purring like a lawnmower.

M was cool too: sweet and kind and seemingly starstruck by me, which no one had ever been before. He made no secret of wanting me. It was a great relief to be wanted. We started hanging out. I graduated from college and began work as a journalist. He stopped smoking pot and went back to college and then on to graduate school. One of the other guys took care of Motorhead.

M and I moved along through many changes, many fits and starts and fights and breakups and reunions until one day, after an argument about something he tearfully asked if I would marry him. Stunned, I said, "Okay." We were twenty-seven and twenty-eight by this time, living in Philadelphia. I was working for the local paper. M was completing graduate school.

Six months after we married we decided to get a dog. That old hey-let's-see-if-we-can-care-for-a-living- thing-without-killing-it-before-considering-kids line of reasoning that people employ. We found Lucy at the local animal shelter. She was the only dog who didn't go insane when we walked in but just sat quietly in her cage, wagging her tail and smiling patiently, as if she had been waiting for us to arrive. She was coal black, maybe thirty pounds, still young, long-nosed and long-legged, part black Lab and part something else. Once we saw her run we guessed that "something else" might be greyhound or whippet. She could run, that dog. She was gorgeous to watch.

She was also fairly intelligent, unlike some dogs I could mention. She walked in the woods with me without running off or getting lost, stayed where you told her to stay, detected friend from foe. She never followed me around the house, just stationed herself as sentry by the front door and waited until I called. She was there if I needed her. She was there when we moved from Philadelphia to White Plains and there when we brought home our daughter and there when we brought home our son and there when we moved from White Plains to Boston and bought a house and put the kids in preschool and found jobs and the marriage fell apart. Somewhere along the way she developed these strange, bulbous growths on her leg. The vet said it was cancer, though now, in painful retrospect, I think he may have been a hack. He said we could possibly carve it out with an expensive operation and then blast it with expensive chemotherapy and if we were any kind of loving dog owners of course that's what we would do, but I was still enough of the child of welfare to consider spending $7,000 on an aging, pampered dog nearly obscene. Even if we had the money. Which we did not.

So the bumps grew and the marriage faltered. We walked the dog and fed her and loved her and kept trying to make things work for the sake of the kids. Trying and failing and trying and failing again. One day I came home from work to find M in teary, whispered conversation with his mother, who was visiting. The next day Lucy started to bleed.

Had I not been reeling, had I been able to think straight I might have saved her life. Had I not been in a stunned, protective crouch I might have seen the vet for the hack he probably was and taken her for a second opinion. Things might have turned out differently. For her.

Instead we wrapped a towel around her bleeding leg and rushed her off to the vet again, who said it was time to either have the surgery or put her down. Maybe he was just trying to bluff us but we were too blindsided to be bluffed. We put her down, then staggered home, sobbing, dazed.

Lucy was thirteen years old when she died. She lasted almost exactly as long as my marriage. Maybe you see why I wasn't keen to get another dog.

**

So that's one thing. But the truth is that even before the divorce I worried about what damage I was doing to my children.

That parents do damage to their children is, in some ways, inevitable. Anyone who thinks otherwise is kidding himself. The only difference is one of degree: a scratch or a dismembering, a cold or the bubonic plague. Or a cold to a person with a weakened immune system, which is the same thing.

In many ways I reached competency early. By the time my son Alex came along, two and a half years after his sister, I knew how to do many things. I knew how to change diapers and burp babies, how to install a car seat like a professional and cut a child's hair so he did not look like a refugee. I knew how to set schedules and keep them, how to encourage their little brains to grow through reading and experiences and limiting that precious-babysitter TV. I knew how not to panic when the blood was gushing from a son who would need stitches, or when a daughter shivered so fiercely her little lips turned a striking shade of blue.

I knew how to check homework and advocate with the teacher and the school system, how to schedule doctor's appointments and find stimulating summer camps and on and on, so even though I had not learned patience or selflessness or to look at the world through the wondering eyes of a child or any of those other rose-colored things mothers are supposed to know, I still felt competent in every category but one. Love.

Here's an example.

One day a few years back my daughter Grace did something that pissed me off. I'd been running around all day, as usual, fifty or sixty balls tumbling through the air and about to drop. I'd been dealing with bosses and deadlines and bills and other adult concerns and then it was time to pick the children up from school and rush my daughter to her orthodontist appointment, where I would shell out some ridiculous amount of cash to straighten teeth that were already better than my own.

When we got to the appointment, however, Grace found out that she was not, as I had told her, getting braces that actual day. She would get them the following week. No big deal—except it meant she had to go back to school the following morning without the braces she had bragged about getting (braces having become, mysteriously in this generation, a declaration of maturity and a source of pride instead of embarrassment). She would have to face the mean girl brigade. This, naturally, embarrassed and worried her. She burst into tears, stomped down the stairs, hurled accusations my way. *Why did I tell her the wrong thing? How could I make such a terrible mistake? Why oh why was I messing with her life?*

Now this is typical, pre-adolescent behavior, and I know much worse is yet to come. I should have laughed it off but instead, I got furious. I stomped right down the stairs behind her, pulling my poor son along. I raised my voice. I yelled at her. I wanted, with all my heart, to make her cringe.

Most people would be happy for another week to eat bagels and candy, why are you crying, I get so sick of you guys crying every time I turn around, it drives me nuts, if this is the worst thing that ever happens to you, you'll be lucky if I had ever spoken to my mother this way she would have smacked me from here to kingdom come! Etc.

Even as I was yelling some part of me realized that my anger was all out of proportion to the misdeed at hand. But I continued. I could not, would not stop myself. I yelled until she cringed.

These maternal moments of madness worry me. I know mothers are only human, that just because a woman pops out a child doesn't mean she turns automatically into a saint. I know too that just because a person came out of your womb doesn't mean they will never get on your nerves.

I mean, everybody gets on my nerves at some point; I could live in a house with the Dalai Lama, Gandhi and Mother Teresa and I'm sure at some point I'd want to pop each of them upside the head. That's the nature of human relationships: friction and joy.

But I can get so angry at my children, so teeth-grittingly pissed that it makes me wonder sometimes if I should have become a mother at all. Am I constitutionally fitted for this job? Was I set in a non-maternal mold early on and now it's too late to reshape the cast? Should there be some kind of standardized test that roots out people who never learned the needed lessons for the job?

But those are all pretty labored metaphors. Here's what it really is: Do I have enough love to give my children? Do I have all the love they need?

**

The kids cry and cry and cry for Lucy, for Lucy and their fractured lives. Their bewilderment and fear makes me want to crawl into a hole and claw dirt over my head. Instead I take them for walks and take them for ice cream and lie in bed with them at night and wipe their tears and let them talk and talk and talk.

After a while they stop crying. After a while they seem to move on with the business of being seven and ten. Months pass. The Ex pushes to have his girlfriend meet the children, though I want to give them time to stabilize. We scratch a painful compromise. Grace asks, "Can we get another dog?"

By this time I have also stopped crying for Lucy. I miss her greatly, but I do not miss picking up her shit. Do not miss vacuuming clumps of black dog hair off the furniture. Don't miss having to rush home in the evening to take her for a walk, or not being able to leave town for the weekend without planning for her care. Don't miss the fleas.

"Let's not rush into anything," I tell Grace. "Let's just let that sit awhile."

Months slide into a year. The kids are wary with the girlfriend. We slog our way into a custody routine: kids here, kids there, forced pleasant exchanges. Grace, riding in the back of the minivan as we drive to the grocery store one afternoon, spies a woman walking a muscular, tail-thumping lab the color of butterscotch.

"Can we get a dog?"

By now, for me, Lucy is a sweet but distant memory. The pleasures of doglessness, on the other hand, have become a golden, daily delight. More sleep in the morning! No claw marks on the wooden hallway floor! No holes in the front lawn, or yellowing grass (or worse) in the back. No paying for, and lugging home, big bags of overpriced kibble. No outrageous veterinary bills.

Most of all, having sweet Lucy gone means one fewer living thing dependent upon me, one less soul I have to feed and shelter and teach and nurse and protect and love. I'm out there floundering in the sweeping, gray Atlantic of heartbreak and pain, struggling to keep the kids above water while I swallow big stomachfuls of salty grief myself. It's just me and the kids out there in the middle of the ocean, and so if the dog sinks to the bottom it's a sad relief. I can't take anyone else on my back.

But Grace comes home from the Ex withdrawn and quiet sometimes, and sometimes Alex cries himself to sleep at night.

"Please, Mommy?"

"How about a cat?" I ask, hopefully. "Cats are really cool!"

They don't want a cat. Cats don't lick you in the face. But I take them over to the SPCA and steer them straight into the cat room (away from the dog place) anyway. There must be fifty cats in this feline playground, long-hairs and short-hairs, yellow and gray, tabbies and whatever-else-kind-of-cats-besides-tabbies you find in an animal shelter. They doze and stare and yawn in their cages. One makes a run for the door whenever someone new walks in, while a few come up and rub themselves around our legs. Alex giggles. Grace screams in delight and melts onto a chair so the kittens can swarm her lap.

We choose a laid-back, black-and-white male, about three years old, with a little Charlie Chaplin mustache. The Boston SPCA staff has named him "Whitey." I get the Boston joke but I can't have a cat named "Whitey." *Here, Whitey! Bad, Whitey!*

Yeah. No.

"How about Dominoe?" suggests Alex on the drive home. My smart, beautiful little boy.

Dominoe crawls out of his cardboard box carrier and takes over the house.

My mother was the oldest of ten children, and the only one of her kind. Meaning that she had no "whole" siblings among the large brood her mother eventually produced, only half. Meaning too that her mother did not marry her father, unlike the fathers of her siblings. It took me years to understand what both these facts meant to her. Many too many years.

Her mother was the youngest of her Mississippi farming family, a short, sassy, ambitious and good-looking gal they called Baby Rae. Baby Rae married five times, all told. Baby Rae moved a lot and left things behind sometimes when she did. Baby Rae remains largely an enigma to me. I don't know what she thought or felt about loving men or having their children or leaving both behind. I don't know what she thought or felt about being born poor and black and female in Mississippi in 1919. I don't know what she thought or felt about not getting an education much beyond grade school or working in people's kitchens and bathrooms most of her life or having a daughter who tried to go to college but did not finish, or having grandchildren who did. I don't know much of anything about Baby Rae because we never spent that much time with her as children and she died before it occurred to me to be curious about such things. It was 1991. I was twenty-seven, just engaged and on my way to Africa for an assignment. She was seventy-two and it was colon cancer. Colon cancer is an epidemic among African Americans: black folks in general, and black women in particular, are far more likely to be diagnosed with, and to die from, colorectal cancer than anybody else. The reasons for this are not clear to scientists, but they seem fairly visible to me; I see them walking down the street every time I drive through the Mattapan or Roxbury neighborhoods of Boston. Bad diets from poverty and lack of education, low access to health care, the stress of being a black woman in this society: it's all right there at the bus stop, weary and worn and ticking like a bomb. Right off the top of my head I can think of two friends whose mothers have died from colon cancer. My mother had it too, though she survived, thanks to God and her excellent doctors at

UC Davis and the common sense to have produced college-educated daughters who pushed her original, inept doctor to order a colonoscopy, and then shoved and pushed and agitated for the best possible care. And had the health insurance to pay for it.

My mother was twenty-three when she gave birth to my oldest sister. This also says a lot, given the time period and the expectations for poor little black girls in Memphis. Against all odds, and I mean nearly all of them, my mother had not only finished high school but had gotten herself into college in Knoxville. It was on break from school and while working for a white family in Connecticut that she met my father, a Navy man. Pretty soon she was pregnant and pretty soon they were married and pretty soon she dropped out of school. Pretty soon there was a baby and pretty soon four more of them, including one set of twins. Pretty soon the marriage exploded. Pretty soon she moved back to Memphis to get some family help raising five children on her own. Pretty soon she was working nights at the post office, a good government job with steady pay and solid benefits and she managed to buy a small house for her children, but pretty soon those children were growing up and growing restless and damaged and acting out. Pretty soon she quit her job to stay home and try to keep them from being preyed upon. Pretty soon she fell into a depression. Pretty soon they were pretty poor.

In terms of mothering, my mother was not just Old School but Old Testament. She was of a generation which did not believe in petting up children, in coddling them or stroking them like anxious horses about to balk. She didn't read to us or play with us or make cookies or push us on swings in the park. She didn't take us to the park at all, in fact, since the park was a place for hoodlums and drunkards to gather; people who wanted to avoid trouble stayed at home.

She talked mostly *at* us rather than *to* us (which seemed awful at the time but now....well, how interesting is a ten-year-old anyway?) She did not hug us or kiss us goodnight or ruffle our hair as she passed by. She did not encourage friendships; when my friend Jackie came over to visit we mostly stayed outside. I never had a sleepover in my life. She did not frequent our school plays or field trips or bake sales or teacher conferences, at first because she was too busy and exhausted and later because she was too self-conscious and, I believe, depressed. Also, the expectation that we work hard and do well in school was clear; she didn't need to be checking up on us, especially as it meant dealing with people and especially white people. My mother did not deal.

My mother never said "I love you." My mother rarely mentioned love at all, just as I am guessing it was rarely mentioned to her. I was in my thirties when she began mysteriously began ending phone calls with the phrase, "Mamma loves you," which seems as heartbreakingly close as she can come. I tell her, I love you too.

What she did do was to feed us and shelter us and clothe us and get us to school every morning and send us off to our Uncle Elmo's church on Sundays for spiritual guidance, though she sought none herself. What she did was discipline us as best she could, desperate and determined not to lose us to pregnancy or jail or alcohol or drugs. My mother was mostly stick, little carrot, and we received our fair share of corrections with belt or sapling switch. Such whippings tended to diminish once the child reached twelve or thirteen, at which point either we "had sense enough to do right" or did not. After that it was mostly a verbal form of discipline. Namely, yelling. My mother could yell. I struggle not to yell myself.

What she did do was not abandon us. What she did was stay there in the thick of so much pain and suffering and keep body and soul together until the last of us was out of the house.

Our bodies and our souls, anyway.

**

My dog Stella is stupid. How stupid is she? My dog Stella is so stupid she sometimes forgets what the stairs are for and tries to slide her way up them. So stupid she tries to eat honeybees. So stupid the children sometimes put bacon on her head and wait for her to figure it out. And wait.

My dog Stella is a big scaredy cat. She's afraid of the vacuum cleaner and of thunder and of going out in the rain. She's afraid of the washing machine and the dryer and the dishwasher and any other major appliance that makes a noise. She's afraid of hoses and dust bunnies, and apparently of being more than five feet away from me.

My dog Stella is disloyal. She follows me around the house, but on the street she just switches her little butt for any Tom, Dick or Harry who saunters past. Off leash and hiking in the hills she will abandon me in a flash if some new human appears upon the trail. Every man she meets is her new boyfriend, every woman her new BFF. The first time she ran away from home she ran right into the open door of a house eight blocks away, nearly giving the startled owner a heart attack. If Genghis Kahn and I stood at opposite ends of a football field and both called her, she'd go to whichever one of us smelled the most like meat.

At least Stella has the common decency to be the size of an actual dog instead of a chipmunk on steroids, a rat with an auburn dye and a weave. Must we really Velveteen Rabbit our pets, America? Is our reluctance to leave adolescence behind so powerful we have to drag an entire species into it? Do we have to play with *everything?*

I wish I could tell you that my dog Stella has taught me buckets and buckets about life and love and the true nature of friendship, but in truth all she's taught me is **not** to activate the chip.

They plant these things in the animal's body at the animal shelter. As we walked out the door the veterinarian handed me a yellow pamphlet explaining what it was and why.

"Please consider this. We see so many lost dogs unnecessarily," she said.

I nodded earnestly, took the pamphlet home and stuck it a drawer. It was only a few months later, after Stella's first walk-about lead to hysterics among the kids and hours spent driving the neighborhood before we found her that I reluctantly activated the chip.

That was her first little Houdini. The sixth time she went missing, after three broken "unbreakable" collars and mounting fines from the town animal control officer, I sighed at the broken leash and closed the back door. Pouring myself a cup of coffee I wondered…would it really be so terrible?

But then the animal control officer from a neighboring town telephoned. "Good news, we found your dog!"

"Hooray."

"Yes," the woman agreed. "Good thing she has a chip!"

**

We'd had Dominoe for more than a year when the dog fever kicked up again, infecting mostly my daughter but also spilling over into me. We all loved the cat, loved scratching him under his chin and having him rotate through our beds each evening or sit in our laps while we watched television on the couch. Dominoe turned out to be the friendliest, most personable cat I'd ever known (but still dignified) but he was not a dog.

By now Lucy had been gone for three years and, like the pain of childbirth, the hassles of dog ownership had mysteriously blurred. Maybe it wasn't really *that* painful. Maybe I kinda overstated the case. Besides, wouldn't it be nice to have an eager face waiting at home when the kids were with their father and I crawled home from a long day of classes? To have a friend along as I hiked the hills?

"I really want a dog," said my daughter.

"We'll look," I said. "Just look."

We went to the Massachusetts Society For The Protection of Animals adoption center, which is attached to a state-of-the-art animal hospital that's nicer than almost every human clinic I saw in Africa. This place is like Canyon Ranch for animals; my guess is that at night they all sit around and conspire on ways to keep their cuteness quotient down so they won't ever be forced to leave. And it turned out that the MSPCA, along with the Animal Rescue League and a few other local shelters, were lousy with cats and fairly stocked with rabbits and guinea pigs but only lightly loaded with adoptable dogs. Apparently, New Englanders, unlike my Southern brethren, are vigilant about putting their dogs under the knife.

The only dogs in reliable abundance were pit bulls. Now, I know, all you pit bull lovers out there are crying, "It's the owner, not the animal! Pit bulls are gentle, loving animals who are no more likely to snack on a toddler than any other dog...." Etc. Etc. But, um, no. Just no.

We looked for months, not steadily but every now and then. We took a lot of dogs for walks around the MSPCA grounds to check their personality and compatibility, and because Grace loved doing so. Once we seriously considered a huge, black bear of a dog who must have weighed 125 pounds and was as sweet as jelly beans but had some kind of hip problem that the volunteers warned would require a lot of medical care. And she wouldn't be able to hike in the hills; she was barely able to get off her pillow to walk with us outside.

Another time we considered another older dog, this one a German Shepherd, also slow and tired and sweet. Grace sat for fifteen minutes rubbing the dog's head but when we talked about it in the car afterwards she shook her head resolutely.

"I don't want a dog that's going to die soon. I don't want to go through that again."

At yet another point I looked into adopting from one of the breed-specific rescue organizations. But let me tell you: it's easier to join the CIA than adopt a dog from one of these places. They wanted credit checks, references, criminal background screens, home visits (plural), a large adoption fee and a fenced-in backyard large enough to house a small African village.

Finally, maybe a year after we'd begun looking, someone told me about the city's animal shelter. Unlike the private shelters, this one was funded by public dollars. You can guess what that means; it was a dump. If the MSPCA shelter is Canyon Ranch the Boston City shelter is, well, a homeless shelter. A homeless shelter for dogs.

"Wow," whispered A when we walked in. "This place is sad."

But when we walked through the concrete-floored anteroom into the back, where the walls were lined with cages and the floors had drains and the dogs all howled for attention and love we saw The Dog of Our Dreams. She was a good size - not too big for the kids to handle, not so small as to be confused with a ridiculous toy or a fluffy, overblown rat. The tag on her cage said she was three years old, a mix of Lab and something unknown and fully housebroken. She was jet black just like Lucy and she leapt up on her two hind legs at the sight of us and wiggled her little behind so furiously she created wind.

"Oh, Mom, look at her! She's so cute!" the children cried. "Can we?"

The lone worker at the desk, a distracted, foot-tapping young white guy, said we could take her outside for a walk if we wanted to. Outside in this case was not the manicured and fenced park of the MSPCA but a sloping, concrete driveway and a dirty sidewalk the width of a clothesline. The dog was eager and under-exercised and untrained but she seemed like something even the kids could handle. After walking her up and down the driveway a few times I handed the leash to Grace, who beamed with love.

When we went back inside the shelter the first desk worker had disappeared. In his place sat a tall, skinny young brother, maybe twenty-five or twenty-six, with cornrows running backward from his face and the flat, determined air of a man at the start of a long, tedious shift that he nonetheless intended to do well. I was happy to see him. I am always happy to see young brothers holding down a job, especially those who, by their hairstyles and the dip of their pants and the pump of their walk are indistinguishable from the hundreds hanging out listlessly on the sidewalks and basketball porches and parks and porches of Dorchester and Mattapan. I feel a little tickle of pride and joy that they haven't given up despite the enormous obstacles, haven't cried "Screw you!" to "the system" and thus, of course, also to themselves. Then I feel guilty that I'm so happy, as if seeing young black men racking a paycheck instead of a gun was such an unusual thing, and I wonder if I'm buying into the hysterical media stereotypes about my own young brothers. And then I remember that in the summer of 2011, as I'm writing this, the unemployment rate for black men is nearly twenty percent. And then I get depressed. Also, pissed.

Unlike the kid who had been there before, this new animal shelter guy, who I dubbed The Dog Whisperer in my head, got up from the desk and came out from the little office to greet us. Also unlike the kid who had been there before, he looked me in the eye.

"You don't want this dog," he said. "This dog is crazy."

I was taken aback. "But we just walked her outside. She seems sweet."

He shook his head. "This dog has a problem. Anybody wearing blue comes around, this dog goes nuts. Watch this." He wrapped the dog's leash around his hand a few times, pulling the dog closer and holding him tight. Then he turned toward the office and called, "Larry!"

A tall white man wearing the dark blue collared shirt and blue polyester pants of a Boston animal control officer came out from somewhere and stood near the desk. "What?" Larry asked.

The next thing I knew, The Dog Of Our Dreams had gone Cujo on poor Larry, or tried to anyway; only the strength of the Dog Whisperer held him back. Grace gasped at the barking and snarling; Alex clapped his hands over his ears. I put them behind me and signaled to the Dog Whisperer that he had made his point. He dragged the dog, still snarling, away.

When he returned he said, "Does that to anybody in a blue uniform."

A few months later Alex would say, out of nowhere, "Wait a second? Aren't dogs colorblind?" But at the time it didn't occur to us. All I could see was the dog sinking its fangs into the legs of our mailman; the mailman limping into court; the mailman settling his scarred leg on the couch in our living room with a satisfied smile; me and the kids and the dog fighting for sleeping space in the car.

"I got a better dog for you," said the Dog Whisperer.

He disappeared into a different part of the shelter and came back with a mid-sized, long-haired black dog with patches of caramel-colored fur on her eyebrows and a tuxedo shirt of white fur on her chest.

"She's got two more days till she's cleared," he said. "You can fill out the paperwork and I'll call you when she's ready."

He handed us the leash and went back to his work. We took the dog outside and walked her up and down the sidewalk for a while. Just before we returned her to the Dog Whisperer Grace got down on one knee and gave the dog a hug.

**

I once saw a bumper sticker reading "Motherhood: A Noble Profession." I had to laugh. Motherhood is many things: a job, certainly and a tough one, perhaps the toughest one you'll ever love. Motherhood is a challenge, an expansion and a responsibility. It is a blessing, a burden, and most certainly a gift but it is not a profession, not even the oldest one. There is no education required, no advanced degree, no training or testing or licensing. There are no standards one must meet, no peer review, only minor regulation, which varies from culture to culture and society to society. A lot of people—a LOT of people—get into it without even meaning to, which is not something to be said about, say, medicine. Ever known anyone to get drunk and wake up a gastroenterologist? No.

There's no yearly evaluation or Maternal Aptitude Test or really any way at all to tell how good or bad a job one is doing in the role, not for a long, long time anyway and maybe not even then, although, Lord knows, we hate to acknowledge that possibility. Kids turned out well? Maybe it was you or maybe you just got lucky. Kids turned out like crap? Maybe the same. Theodore Kaczynski had perfectly lovely parents by all accounts. Richard Pryor was raised by prostitutes and violent jerks.

It may seem churlish to make so much of a piece of paper slapped on the back of someone's car. In all likelihood the woman behind the wheel was a stay-at-home mother seeking acknowledgement and respect for her choice in a society which does not always grant as much. We're schizophrenic in this way: we propagate a Cult of The Child, arranging our lives around the little ones, abandoning all adult sense and interaction, denigrating any mother who dares skip out on a soccer game now and then, while at the same time turning our noses just slightly upward at the women who choose to make house and home the center of their lives. No wonder that woman wants to equate her day job with medicine or architecture or law.

Still, it feels important to question this idea of motherhood as a state of being, as somehow inherently noble, or even a natural state toward which every woman should aspire and direct herself. Because this idea still permeates our culture, though we pretend otherwise. And those who don't experience motherhood in this way, not to mention those who never do and are grateful and those who do but end up wondering if they were really meant to, can end up feeling strange, broken, wrecked.

Some days my daughter comes up to where I'm standing and bumps me like a colt. I know what this means: she wants to be hugged. She wants to feel, without having to ask, her mother's arms around her for a few minutes, wants to be embraced and made to feel safe. I do it, of course, though it doesn't come naturally.

We grew up without much touching, unless you count the touch of a switch. (Though, really, my mother switched us only infrequently, and after the age of ten or eleven not at all. I think she was too tired by then.) I never thought about the lack of hugging and kissing and other physical forms of maternal affection much until my own first child was on the way. Early in the pregnancy I decided I would force myself to breastfeed — force being the operative word. Breast feeding was largely foreign to me, despite the La Leche exuberance of my sisters-in- law. As far as I knew, my mother had not breastfed us, my oldest sister had not breastfed her children and neither had any other woman in my family. When I was younger and watching over baby siblings and cousins and other such it was bottle, bottle, bottle all the way. We never really talked about it, but somehow I absorbed the notion that breastfeeding was no longer necessary and slightly disgusting. Nasty, really. In the black Southern sense of that versatile word.

Watching women breastfeed on the video in my child birthing class made me queasy. Watching women do it in public made my stomach curl. When my turn came I knew enough about the health benefits of breastfeeding to the baby involved to bite the bullet, but I did not expect to like it much. I would endure for the sake of my child and her future I.Q.

So I was surprised to discover, once the first hard and painful weeks had passed, how much I liked this oldest way possible of feeding my child. All the stuff women gush about was true: the bonding warmth of it, the closeness, the feeling of accomplishment (and, yes, power) that comes from being able to nourish a human being with only one's body, oneself.

There is a chemical released in a woman's body when she breastfeeds, a chemical called oxytocin which produces feelings of attachment and closeness. (One could argue that all of human love is but hormones and projection, both outside of our control and completely of our own imagining.) Thank God for it because the truth is that I did not fall in love with my daughter at that magical moment of birth, the way normal mothers apparently do. When they handed me that scrunched-faced little bundle with the startling blue(!) eyes I thought: 1) Shit, that hurt and 2) Never doing that again and 3) Can I please get some sleep?

Even after we got home the next day and lay Grace in the center of the bed and stood there looking down at her I felt mostly a strange combination of confusion and numbness and a dulled, creeping sense of fear. Now what was I thinking, again? That this was a good idea? Because it had always looked so wonderful when I was growing up?

What was strange was that I had never particularly desired children, or even marriage. What I wanted was to escape Memphis, to not be poor and to be rapturously, desperately loved. Preferably by David Soul or Marlon Jackson but on this point I was flexible. The marriage and children part were not important, didn't take up a lot of space in my head. Didn't play with dolls growing up. Didn't spend time daydreaming about my perfect wedding. Never bought a bridal magazine in my life.

When M proposed we'd just finished a kind of blowout fight and I said yes mostly because it seemed the thing to do when someone was polite enough to ask. For the first few weeks I carried the engagement ring around in my pocket, pulling it out when I got home. We were married for five or six years (I don't remember) before the idea of reproducing entered my head. By that time I was kind of miserable. I hated my job as a journalist for the New York Times (aka The Great Gray Pit of Vipers). I was in love with someone who was not my husband and who was in love with someone who was not me. Needless to say, M and I were struggling; counseling was only mildly useful. I was, though I did not articulate it as such, sobbingly, angrily, crazily depressed, so depressed it was hard to decipher if things were a mess because of the depression or the depression the result of things being a mess. Either way something had to give. As frightening as it was to consider walking away from a job without having another one, a job which nearly everyone said I'd be flat crazy to leave, it was even more frightening to consider walking away from the only person I thought would ever love me. The only person who ever had. I quit the Times. Started writing a novel. Was home all day without a job for the first time since I was fourteen, and too ashamed to even go to the drugstore until after six o'clock. Thought: hey, might as well have a kid.

"Hear that? That's the heartbeat," said the doctor, rubbing the ultrasound wand across my stomach. I burst into tears. But when my sister came to visit after my daughter was born she said, "Um, where's the crib? Where's the changing table? Where's all the clothes and diapers and bottles and stuff?"

"Yeah. I haven't really gotten to that stuff yet," I told her.

I had a bassinet, a gift from M's mother and a few onesies from a baby shower and some diapers from the hospital.

"Most people would have spent months preparing the nursery," my sister pointed out. I just shrugged.

I didn't really fall in love with my daughter until the third or fourth week of her young life, when her tiny, piercing cry would drag me from bed at 3 a.m. and I'd lift her from the bassinet and stagger into the living room and turn on the television and sit in the rocking chair and hold her in my arms and to my breast while *Hill Street Blues* played with my heart. I think it was breastfeeding that saved me as mother. As much as I was saved.

Still, by nine months, when my daughter started to lose interest and the hormone high began to wane, I was ready to let it go. I was ready to take my body back. To not be so constantly touched.

Things only intensified when my son came along. Suddenly there were two little people, both voraciously clamoring to be held, to be hugged, to be changed and diapered and picked up and put down and brushed off and bathed and washed. Some days, walking to the park or to the car or to the store, my daughter, three years old and sensing displacement by the baby, would grasp automatically for my hand and I would have to force myself to let her take it. If it was a question of safety, of crossing the street or navigating a busy parking lot or a cavernous store that was one thing: I grabbed those little fingers and I held on tight and that was simply that.

But sometimes, just walking along the smooth and open path at the park she would want to hold hands and I'd let her, but only for a minute. I'd squeeze and let go. She grabbed again, talking all the while, on autopilot, and I let her hold a little longer this time but then I'd find something to distract her and let go again. She grabbed. I held and relinquished. The pattern repeats.

I know my mother loved us. I know my mother loved us because she sacrificed every hope and every dream she ever held for herself that we might live and even prosper. I know this now and it breaks my heart.

Still, I cannot say, cannot honestly say, I ever *felt* loved when I was little. Holding my daughter in my arms I wonder: is it the being loved or the feeling loved that matters most?

**

Delivering the news of one's divorce is like handing your friends and neighbors a Rorschach test. What they see in that blotch of spilled life has everything to do with them and nothing to do with you.

Remember that. Otherwise, the shit people say will hurt.

"I didn't even know you guys were having trouble!"

"Did you think of counseling?"

"Have you thought about what this means for the children?"

"Who cheated - you or him?"

"Wow, that's the third one I've heard of this month! It's like a disease around here. I hope it isn't contagious!"

The proper responses to these statements, sadly unavailable to me at the time because all my energy was being diverted into not shattering into bits when I stepped from the house, are as follows:

Sorry, didn't you get the newsletter?

Nah. I saw those socks on the floor and thought: to heck with this.

Children? What children? Shit!

Wow. I'm going to pretend you did not just reveal something sad and painful about yourself.

Me too. Because then you'd be a rude, insensitive asshole *and also* divorced.

People mean well, of course. People almost always mean well, and the road to hell is paved with their splatterings. People want to comfort and to soothe and most of all, to make you stop hurting, because your pain is uncomfortable to them. People do not want to sit in the same room as pain. Sitting next to pain is painful, and frightening. Sitting still beside pain reminds us that no one gets out of this thing unscathed. Which is depressing. Better to just say something and make it stop.

"Children are resilient. They'll be fine."

"As long as the parents are happy the kids will be happy also."

"Hey, I wish my parents had gotten a divorce when I was a child!"

This is utter rubbish, all of it. Well-intentioned, well-meaning crap.

No child wants his parents to split. Maybe he wants Daddy to stop hitting Mommy, or Mommy to stop drinking and blaming it on Dad or all the yelling or sniping or crying to cease, but that doesn't mean they want that at the expense of both parents in the house loving them. And as for children being happy as long as their parents are—that is such self-gratifying American tripe. Up to a certain age children are utterly oblivious of your happiness. Up to a certain age children don't notice your unhappiness at all as long as their needs are being met.

What they want is for their world to remain stable, for their needs to be met, for what has been to continue to be. What they want is Mom and Dad and any other available adult around to love them, and, yeah, sure, to love one another too, that's nice when it happens but hey. They want Mommy and Daddy holding hands not because it makes Mom and Dad happy but because it makes them feel safe and secure. Children are selfish. So are adults.

Divorce wounds children. There is no getting around this painful fact, no rolling down the sleeve and pretending that all is well; amputation may be necessary but it will surely leave a scar. The best you can do, having weighed the damage of cutting versus the damage of allowing the diseased limb to remain, is to make it swift and surgical. Then saturate the wound with balm and bandage as best you can.

So you build a working relationship with the father of your children, and you count your blessings that somehow, despite it all, you picked for the father of your children a decent man. You pretend not to see his missteps and foibles during the process. You bite your tongue until grooves run deep. You figure out a way to make some extra money so you can stay in the house. You remain in a city you hate because he is there and he's their father and that city is the only home they've ever known.

And you get a dog.

**

So, let's start again.

Yesterday I got pissed at my daughter. I was having a bad day for lots of nonsense reasons, unimportant, and then I was supposed to just shift all that to the side and focus on the needs of my children and I couldn't do it. Not seamlessly. Or maybe I didn't want to do it, not at that moment, not on call, which is what motherhood demands. In that moment I didn't want to be the mother, didn't want to have to walk with my daughter through the slings and arrows of adolescent girlhood (again!), didn't want to have to care about her emotional needs.

We drove home in silence, and she ran up to her room. I went into the kitchen, poured myself a cup of orange juice, drank it down for fortification.

Had I been my mother, that would have been the end of it. If her generation did not believe in petting children, it also did not much believe in sitting down to discuss things, especially emotional moments. Giving the children a good talking to, absolutely. But listening to what they had to say or how they were feeling? Considering it? Maybe even apologizing in the end?

Right.

Someone said to me once, "You're a good mother" and I just laughed because I know good and damn well that I am not. A good mother is so far out of my reach it's not even amusing. A good mother is like Jupiter.

What I hope to be is a good enough mother. What I hope to be is just a better mother than my mother. Not because my mother was a terrible mother but getting ever-better is the point, isn't it? Every generation improves. We usually take this to mean materially, but that's not important, really. The material stuff. Not by comparison.

My mother was not loved as a child. Or maybe she was loved a little, but she sure as hell was not loved enough. Not nearly enough, and not by the people from whom she wanted it most. I know this now though I didn't growing up myself. My mother was left behind by her own mother, and so later, when it came time for her to do the mothering herself, she made sure she stayed. She refused to abandon us, though staying would, in the end, cost her a great deal.

Still, she stayed and that was huge, though we didn't understand it then. She did not leave when things got bad, when the marriage to my father fell apart and she lost her job and poverty settled in. Not when the days became mostly about clawing and scraping to survive with five demanding children. She remained. It was both the least and the most that she could do. It was everything.

But lovelessness always leaves its mark. In the neighborhood of our lives lovelessness is the first spray of graffiti, the first shattered glass. The worse the neighborhood looks the more people stay away; the more people stay away, the worse the neighborhood becomes. Lovelessness leaves a mark which makes it harder to get love and to receive it, which leaves a mark, which makes it harder, and round and round. The people who most need love, the ones with the biggest holes in their hearts from childhood hurts are the ones least likely to get it, because those same hurts create in them attributes and personalities that frighten or drive love away. How fair is that? But this is life, isn't it? Life don't care from fair.

The song says, "Them that's got, shall get. Them that's not, shall lose."

I was thinking: what a different person my mother would have been had just one person in her life loved her deeply at some critical moment, some formative time. And what different people my sisters and brother and I would have been, because our mother would have been different in raising us. And what a different mother my children would have, someone more patient and forgiving perhaps, someone less critical and, yes, even resentful at times. What a different mother for them and maybe they too would be different and their children and so on and so on. Lovelessness rolls downhill, gathering momentum, breaking roots and splintering hearts.

My daughter pissed me off and I resented her ingratitude, but I came home and regrouped. Took a breath. Had some orange juice. Went upstairs to her room. I had to make myself do it. That's the truth: I was not feeling love at that moment, no maternal tenderness creased my brow. But one thing I have learned is that love is a verb. It's something you do, not something you have. I wasn't feeling love, but I could act it anyway.

I went up to my daughter's room and knocked on her door and went inside and sat down on the bed next to her and put my arm around her shoulders and apologized. Said I was sorry I had yelled. Explained that I was tired and overstressed. Said I understood she was just disappointed. She was worried about how her friends would react, and friends, at that age, are everything, every, single frickin' thing. Made some suggestions for handling the situation. Hugged her again and made her smile.

Some days I think this may be my only role here: to stop this avalanche of lovelessness, to save my children. If I can love them enough, though not perfectly, they may grow up to find and give their own love, and on and on —the cycle broken, a better cycle born.

Lovelessness rolls downhill, gathering momentum. Lovelessness rolls downhill, breaking roots and splintering branches, wiping out everything in its path, but one person can stop it. One person can raise his hand and stop the rolling. One person can bend and catch it in her heart.

IV:
TRAIN UP A CHILD

The obvious parable to begin with here would be the one about the prodigal son.

You know: a father foolishly gives his two sons their inheritance before he dies. Son number one dutifully stashes it and goes right back out in the fields and gets to work, doing whatever his father tells him to. Son number two takes the bundle and runs off to a foreign land, where he squanders his inheritance on wine, women and song and soon finds himself working as a swineherd and envying the pigs. He decides to return home and beg his father's forgiveness, offering to work as a common laborer on his father's lands.

But the father, seeing his lost son returned to him, welcomes him with great feasting and celebration. He gives him a new robe and new shoes, kills the fatted calf and throws a party to outdo them all. Which naturally pisses off the brother who has stayed behind and done the work. He goes to Dad and complains. In response the father says to him, "Son you are always with me, and all I have is yours. It was right that we should make merry and be glad, for your brother was dead and is alive again, and was lost and is found."

Here's the thing to remember about that prodigal child, the thing that often gets overlooked or misinterpreted: he never repudiated his father. He didn't spit on the ground, dust off his hands, turn his back. He just turned his face in a different direction, wandered off to see what else the world had to give. When he saw what that was he turned around and came home again. That doesn't mean he never sits out on the pasture fence at sunrise and wonders, wonders and yearns. It just means he decided it was not worth the trip.

**

My kids and I have a tradition; every fall we go for a walk in the woods and chase leaves. I don't remember where this ritual came from, or who decided that catching a falling leaf before it hit the ground was good luck. All I know is their father and I used to do it before they were born, when we were young and hopeful and open ourselves.

Being me (meaning: Southern, black, daughter of Ethel) somewhere along the line I managed to twist this silly game into something else, something suspiciously like superstition, in which catching a leaf was good luck and failing to catch at least one leaf per fall was naturally the opposite. Bad luck to go home leafless. Bad luck to face the looming winter without at least one saved leaf drying on the mantelpiece, one piece of tangible grace to get me through the dangerous months.

So one morning recently when I decide to take the dog for a hike in the Blue Hills not far from my house I think I might also catch a leaf or two. It is a beautiful fall day in New England, postcard-perfect with the sky the color of the fat morning glories which climb my neighbor's fence, and the leaves are just beginning to turn. A day to be happy to be alive but I am not, particularly. I am depressed.

I am depressed. I hate even writing that, hate the admission of moral failing, a finding of self-fault, like *I am drunk* or *I am ungroomed* and sloppily dressed. I am in a state I could alter or avoid if I just tried hard enough, did the right things, became the right kind of person. Looked at life the appropriate way. Snapped the fuck out of it.

Deep down inside this is the way we feel about people with depression, despite all the sad-eyed women on drug commercials winding up doll versions of themselves. God knows it's the way many black people feel. One sister tells me to get more sun and drink more water. Another tells me to read the Bible and pray. All the women at church second this suggestion: depression is not anger turned inward or a biochemical imbalance or a reasonable response to a cold and heartless world but simply a lack of faith. Which makes it practically a sin. To be depressed means your faith is weak, your belief built on shifting sand. And whose going-to-hell fault was that?

Taken to an extreme this leads to the tragedies of people with schizophrenia or bipolar disorder or any number of serious illnesses going undiagnosed and untreated except for prayer and stern lectures and the occasional exorcism. But we don't even have to go that far to consider the damage of disbelieving in mental illness. We can, for example, look at me.

I am fifteen and staggering around the campus of my fancy New England boarding school like one of the walking dead. "Smile!" people order, scurrying past.

"Smile!" they demand and I would gladly acquiesce except the scowl on my face is the only thing keeping me from shattering into bits. When a black teacher, one of two or three at the school, encounters me on the path and asks if I'm okay, I burst into hysterical tears.

"You should see someone," he urges. "A counselor."

I am appalled at the suggestion. "That's white people's mess!" I bark, disappointed and disgusted. After all, he's black: he should know better. "No thanks," I declare and go on suffering, black and proud.

Which is ridiculous. Because if any group of people in America stands in desperate need of mass therapy it is black people. White people too, of course. White people in America are all kinds of sick. White people in Europe and Africa too. I can't speak to Asians (or South Asians or Southeast Asians) though from casual, pop cultural observation I'd guess there's plenty of good room for deep examination in those cellars as well. Latinos too, I'd guess: I know enough Dominicans (and have read enough Junot Diaz) and Puerto Ricans and Mexicans and, Lord knows, Cubans to peek some of that mess. So, yeah, just about everybody in America could use mass therapy. But I'm interested in my own.

Anybody not crazy can see that black people in America are the walking wounded, psychologically. Three hundred and fifty years of brutal physical, psychological and emotional oppression? Fifty years of an easing of that oppression, but a continued war on drugs and poverty/ war on poor people and a Jim Crow prison system? Internalized racism that continues to manifest in all kinds of nonsense about what's beautiful and desirable and what is not. Half a trillion dollars a year on straightening and weaving our hair (yeah, I said it.) One in nine African American men under the age of 34 behind bars. The sisters I hear on the subway, loudly calling one another bitch and 'ho'.

To his nephew James Baldwin wrote, "You can only be destroyed by believing that you really are what the white world calls a nigger. I tell you this because I love you, and please don't forget it."

But we have. So many of us.

Me, I pull myself off the couch and head out with the dog. At the trailhead the parking lot stands empty, a great relief. It means I can let this crazy hound off her leash to run and, if nothing else, she will get the exercise she needs. During the week she gets a few minutes in the yard in the morning, a fifteen-minute walk at the end of the day. This is insufficient; she is long and leggy and needs much, much more. Also food and water and flea protection and medicine for Lyme disease and to have her anal sacs squeezed (seriously?) and to be petted and bathed and loved. The kids need too, all kinds of things, material and spiritual and emotional and more. Some days I feel as if I am drowning in the needs of other beings but then, I asked for it, didn't I?

At the top of the first incline up from the parking lot I unleash the dog and she flies off down the trail, giddy and free. I follow, forcing myself to look up at the sky and the leaves, to notice the astonishing beauty of the natural world, to breathe deep the crisp, earthy air. The pines shower down a steady rain of golden needles. The maples are muted and already half-bare, the birches a steady yellow, the other trees still strangely, dully green. It was a wet summer and thus a disappointing early fall. Snap out of it.

I will catch a leaf. It will stand as a sign, a reminder that things won't feel this way forever, this howling loneliness will someday ease.

The Blue Hills are laced with trails. I choose one which takes nearly an hour if I'm moving steadily and even running when the trail is flat. But today the trails are wet and muddy; I forgot about all that rain earlier in the week. The dog sluices straight through the impermanent creeks and transient streams that water the downhill trails, but I'm wearing sneakers instead of boots and so I pick my way around, slowing progress. Every time a leaf falls in my sight I rush after it, trying not to slog through puddles or stumble over tiny boulders or fall face-down onto sharp outcroppings of slate and hard, New England rock. I'm not having much luck. Though the day is breezy and the wind high the leaves cling stubbornly to their branches, unwilling to fall. When they do release it always seems to be just ahead or just behind, too far off the trail or too deep in the mud. Or the wind catches it just as I stretch out my hand and slaps it to the ground.

You have to catch them before they hit the ground or else it doesn't count.

Halfway round the loop we meet an older couple and their two dogs. She is tiny and dark-haired and spectacled; he wears a baseball cap and his sweatshirt tied around his waist. One dog is a black lab with a graying muzzle and the other some tiny, snippy thing who circles Stella and barks. Altogether they are the picture of romantic contentment, mellowed domestic bliss. Stella plays for a while, then we walk on. I am still leafless. Three-quarters of the way and I veer from my usual route to climb above the tree line and catch a view across to the Great Blue Hill. I will my heart to life at the sight of it, demand that my spirit gets its lazy ass out of bed and pulls up the blinds. See? See? See!

Yeah. Okay. Nice.

Three-quarters of the way around I slow my pace, determined not to leave these woods without a leaf. In a clearing within sight of my car I pause and run around for five minutes or so, chasing the brittle, browning bombs. Every single one blows just out of my reach. A group of four older white people come up the hill and startle at the sight of me. Usually I'd smile to put them at ease but right now I don't give a damn. I want that leaf.

The dog takes off after the old people. I have to chase her to get her back. Leaves rain down, teasing me. I can't catch them so I catch the dog and leash her. My heart leaks. I give up.

If the dog weren't pulling me forward I would sit down in the dirt and not get up again. Can't catch leaf, can't catch love, hah hah. Can't catch leaf, can't catch love, makes perfect sense. I know this is ridiculous but still I start to cry.

I head down to my car, get within sight of it. The dog tugs. I reach into my pocket for my keys ... and feel something smack me in the face. Naturally, it's a leaf.

A beech, I think, more brown than yellow, more ripped than whole but with those funky little notches and a tiny, perfect hole kissing one of the veins and the petiole where it once clung to the branch still intact. It smacks right into my cheek, the stem very nearly poking me in the eye. I grab it. Then I laugh.

Does God exist? Do I believe? Most days I yearn to answer that question without hesitation, to stand and deliver an unequivocal yes: yes, I believe, yes, I know my redeemer lives. There are people I know, people I love and admire whose faith is unshakable, who stand on solid ground in this regard. These folks I envy. So hard it's a sin.

Does God exist? Do I believe? Some days I want to answer no, to be rid of this hovering question, to dismiss with a wave of my progressively educated blue state hand such a ridiculous notion. There are people I know, people I respect and love whose non-faith is as uncomplicated as laundry, as neatly tucked as a tuxedo shirt. These friends I do not so much envy as half-expect (and half-fear) to reluctantly someday join, like AARP. Unquestioning faith, unquestioning atheism, it's all the same. Certainty is certainty and human minds like certainty; who wants medicine when they can have milk? What I want more than anything is certainty, and since it's easier to talk oneself out of faith than into it, this would seem to be the way to go.

Only, for the life of me, I can't.

Not from fear or superstition or childhood indoctrination but from...something. Some yearning. Some feeling. Some inability to dismiss my own experience.

Every now and then, a broken leaf smack in the face.

God says: "Here. Here, okay? Happy? Can I get back to the Middle East?"

**

I am twenty-nine and curled on the gray-carpeted floor of a furnished apartment in midtown Manhattan, sobbing like a motherless child. I am not quite sure why I'm sobbing, other than the desperate unhappiness. And the howling loneliness. And the gnawing despair. Other than that.

In a few minutes the telephone will ring. It will be the therapist I have been seeing off and on, off and on for maybe a year. She lives outside of Philadelphia, where I also, technically live, at least on the weekends, in a house with M and the dog we got. On the weekdays I live here in this sterile, white-walled place in midtown Manhattan with the cheap Ikea couch and the windows overlooking Broadway that admit so much noise I cannot sleep at night. The therapist believes my problem is my father did not love me as a child and so I seek approval and love from men wherever I may go, and then, not finding it, or not finding enough, get depressed. Since she is tall and honey-blonde and wears white cashmere stirrup pants tucked into high-heeled boots and has her office in the downstairs back of her giant brick Colonial with the sweeping circular driveway in Bryn Mawr (which at first I think is dangerously foolish but later realize is perfectly okay: she's not seeing anyone dangerous) and since the rock on her hand blinds me when she forgets to pull down the shade, I can see that she has been adored and loved since the moment she first slicked out of the womb. I want to say, do say, "What the hell do you know about it, anyway?" She says she understands. I snort in derision. The only reason I keep talking to her is because I am afraid to stop.

The only reason I keep talking to her is because there are times when I feel that if I don't talk to someone, if I don't run out onto the sidewalk and grab some human being by the collar and cry, "Listen to me! Listen to me! For God's sake, please listen to me!" and if he nonetheless fails to listen I will do something desperate. What that something desperate is I do not allow myself to think.

**

"Train up a child in the way he should go and when he is old he will not depart from it," says the Bible. If I heard that passage quoted once when I was younger, I heard it a thousand times: thundered down from the pulpit or admonished by the royal-crowned mothers of the church as they lined us up for Sunday school. "Train up a child in the way he should go." One third promise, one third threat, one third piece of parenting advice. Train up a child, they said with certainty and hope but every time I heard that passage a small, still voice inside my small and childish heart snorted an objection: "Just wait, just you wait."

I was born and raised in Memphis and in the Church of God in Christ, which, if you are black, is virtually the same thing. The Church of God in Christ is a Pentecostal or Holiness church, meaning a church which ascribes primary importance to the Biblical events on the day of Pentecost, fifty days after Passover and ten days after Christ ascended into heaven.

The Bible says, "And when the day of Pentecost was fully come, they were all with one accord in one place. And suddenly there came a sound from heaven as of a rushing mighty wind, and it filled all the house where they were sitting. And there appeared unto them cloven tongues like as of fire, and it sat upon each of them. And they were all filled with the Holy Ghost, and began to speak with other tongues, as the Spirit gave them utterance."

Pentecostal churches consider this event the birthday of the Christian church and one that should be manifested in those who properly worship God. The Church of God In Christ in particular declares, in its official doctrine, that the Baptism of the Holy Ghost is an experience subsequent to conversion and sanctification and that tongue-speaking is the consequence of that baptism. A Holy Ghost experience is necessary to be saved. Mandatory, is the word.

This was where the problem began.

What must I do to be saved?

The good things about growing up in the Pentecostal church were the incredible music, the very real spirit of celebration and community which swept over the church most Sundays and the genuine love of the people in the pews for one another. And the food after service. The food was rocking.

The bad things were the Puritanical restrictions, the crushing condemnation and pervasive spirit of judgment, the presentation of God as an outraged Father to be placated and feared. Also the length of any given service. If there is one thing the saints of the Church of God in Christ know how to do it is to have church. All. Day. Long.

Three hours was the bare minimum, and any service which achieved that level of brevity and efficiency was noteworthy. More common were services that stretched to three and a half hours or even to four. Church usually began, after some spirited singing and the welcome, with testimony service. Anyone so moved was allowed to stand up and testify to the good things God had done for them that week, or to ask for prayers for things that maybe weren't going so well.

Now I understand that for many of these women, who spent their days working in somebody's kitchen or hospital room or high school cafeteria or nursing home, Sunday was the one chance all week they got to dress up and look up instead of down. And testimony service was the chance within that chance to be not only seen but heard. Now I see the human hunger manifest in this tradition. Back then I was just bored out of my skull.

Every now and then my mother would make one of us testify, which might as well have been making us dance naked in the school cafeteria. The trick was to stand up quick, not look at anyone but especially the stained-glass picture of Jesus above the altar, white face aglow, and to get it over as quickly as possible:

"Giving honor to God and to the pulpit and to all the saints of the church I'd just like to thank the Lord for bringing me and my family safely through this week and for blessing us and I ask your prayers that the Lord may continue to bless us richly."

Then plop your butt back down in the pew to a chorus of "Amen!"and approving nods. Done and done.

After testimony came more singing and praising, then the announcements and presentations (black people love presentations, and Southern black church people especially) and welcoming of guests, which could easily chew through another hour or so. Especially if the guest was a visiting preacher, in which case he (and it was always a he) would be invited to bring a greeting to the church. Which was like inviting a lion to bring a greeting to the lambs.

Then the sermon. The choir,-having performed its soul-softening duty, fluffs its collective robes and takes a seat. The preacher, wiping his face with a snow-white handkerchief and toting a Bible as big as his chest, climbs into the pulpit and raises his eyes. Out in the congregation women slip off their shoes and take up their Martin Luther King Jr. fans. Everybody get good and comfortable. We are going to be here for a while.

This was my cue to start daydreaming. While the preacher thundered about sin and hell and fire and brimstone and the wickedness of gin and card-playing and premarital sex and women in general (oddly enough I don't remember ever hearing a sermon preached against homosexuality. In fact, I barely remember homosexuality or homosexuals even being mentioned when I was a child, which is interesting. Of course anyone who was openly gay probably would have been either shunned or prayed over, but in general the black church seemed a lot less obsessed with the topic then than it is now) I would slink down in the pew, glaze my eyes and drift.

Some days I think the Church of God in Christ was God's way of turning me into a writer. *Here you go, my child: learn to live in your head.*

At some point we stopped attending Temple and started going instead to the small storefront church of my Uncle Elmo. Uncle Elmo was actually my mother's uncle, baby brother to my grandmother, and during the week he worked at some job I never really knew but on Sundays he was called to preach The Word.

If anything Uncle Elmo's church was even more fundamentalist than our old one: we came to understand that just about anything we did or wanted to do or even thought about was coated in wickedness and sinfulness. There was fornication, of course. Listening to secular music. Cursing or smoking. Playing cards. Wearing pants or other men's clothing, not just to church but anywhere (to this day I will not wear pants to church). Disrespecting our elders. Lipstick. Beer.

On Saturdays Uncle Elmo would sometimes pick us up from home and drive us to his church to clean. We swept the floor and wiped down the pews and cleaned the bathroom, but the one time I started to go up into the pulpit to dust the podium he stopped me.

"Not up there!" he bellowed, waving me away. "Not you! Leave it be for someone else!"

Later I asked one of the older teenagers in the church, a girl who always wore her skirts the proper length and never touched makeup and swayed and cried mysteriously when souls were being saved why Uncle Elmo had freaked out so. What had I done?

"Women ain't allowed in the pulpit," she explained patiently, as though this were obvious. "Not to preach and not even to stand. You might be unclean."

"But I took a bath this morning."

She gave me a look, swirled her head from side to side to see if anyone was listening, and lowered her voice. "You might be having your time of the month."

"Oh." I flushed. I knew what she meant, and I knew that being on my period was, somehow disgusting to other people and especially to men. But I hadn't known God felt that way too.

"Well, I'm not. Not right now," I managed to say.

She shrugged. "He don't want to ask, so he just banned all women from being in the pulpit. The Bible says a woman having her time of the month is unclean and anything she touches becomes unclean too."

This was terrifying news. "Every time?"

She nodded. "For seven days. And after you have a baby, if it's a boy you're unclean for forty days and if it's a girl you're unclean for eighty days."

My head was spinning. "Oh. Okay."

To make the lesson stick she quoted some scripture. "Let the woman learn in silence with all subjection. But I suffer not a woman to teach, nor to usurp authority over the man, but to be in silence. For Adam was first formed, then Eve. Adam was not deceived, but the woman being deceived was in the transgression. First Timothy, two and eleven."

"Okay."

By now I didn't want to clean the pulpit anymore, or even think about doing so. All I wanted was to go home. If God thinks you're disgusting, you're pretty much screwed.

What I remember most about the churches of my childhood was how I felt walking into them and how I felt walking out, which was this: guilty, terrified, coated with sin. What I rarely felt in either of those two buildings was at home. What I rarely felt was God's all-abiding love. I know somebody must have actually mentioned the word; I know somebody at some point must have stood in either of those pulpits and talked about God's love for us, for me. But for some reason I never heard it or felt it or carried it. God hated me, that's what I got from church. He was disappointed and disgusted and pissed. Really, really pissed.

Did I believe? It wasn't really a question of belief. God was a fact, like the blaze of the Memphis sun in August. Regardless of what I believed, if I went outside and ran around I was going to sweat. And if I didn't get saved before I died—which could happen at ANY MINUTE— I was going to hell.

This was nearly as terrifying as the alternative, which was being saved and involved standing in front of the church and being attacked by the Holy Ghost. I did not disdain the process; it was stark and astonishing and powerful. I just couldn't ever see myself doing it.

By the age of twelve I was pretty much resigned to my doom.

**

I am thirty-one and taking Prozac. My ob-gyn, the doctor I see most often, has prescribed them for me at my request, only a few questions asked. "Do you feel sad or depressed most of the day and has this feeling lasted at least two weeks? Do you feel a loss of enjoyment in things that were once pleasurable? Any fatigue or loss of energy? Insomnia or excessive sleep? Recurring thoughts of death or suicide?"

Yes, yes, yes, I answer. Kinda, sorta and what the hell do you think I'm doing here? Can I have the frickin pills, already? Can I have the frickin pills?

"Sometimes depression manifests itself as anger," she remarks, scribbling in her notes.

I look around the room for blunt objects to throw.

"You might consider seeking counseling." She rips off the script. "The pills are not a cure-all."

Thanks and get the hell out of here so I can get out of this paper dress and back into my clothes.

At first the drugs don't seem to be working. I still open my eyes each morning with a sigh of bewilderment, still trudge through the day like a man trudging off to war. I still lie down in the evening exhausted and wondering, "What was the point of all that anyway?" I still cry a lot. And cry and cry and cry.

Then, gradually, slowly, it seems that they are. Instead of swimming through quicksand I'm moving through currents of water, cold and swift but clear. I get out of bed without feeling defeated, have more patience with M and his human foibles, have more patience with everyone. I go two days without crying and then four and then eight.

I also cannot write.

It's not coming. No matter how hard I try it will not come. Digging for words becomes like trying to excavate a hidden city with the back of a comb. I can't write, I don't want to write, nothing's pushing me to do so. I sit on my bed with my laptop on my desk and stare out at the sky. Hours pass. I close the laptop lid.

"It's empty," I tell M. "I guess I feel better but it's empty. There's nothing there."

He is torn. I can see it. No one wants to live with a desperate, desperately-angry woman. Still, he
says, "Maybe you have to stop taking the pills."

I stop taking the pills.

**

"Wanna go to church?"

I look up from my bowl of Raisin Bran. Janine stands next to the table, holding her own empty tray and smiling at me.

"Sure," I say, though of course I do not. It is my third or fourth weekend at this strange, new boarding school in a strange new state (New Hampshire) in a strange new part of the world (New England) and I am reeling. But the one thing I had counted on actually liking about being miraculously admitted to a fancy institution I'd never heard of, packed up against my will by my determined mother and flown a thousand miles away to the frozen north all by myself was not having to go to church.

Still, Janine and the thimbleful of other black upperclass women tossing around this cooling campus have been my lifeline in this strange and terrifying storm. If she wants me to go to church I will. Actually, maybe I'm supposed to go to church anyway. Maybe we're required to and I've already screwed up?

I look around the dining hall, with its slanting ceiling and exposed red brick walls and sharp angles and china cabinets and design by some famous guy I have never heard of before. It is now half-empty; laughter echoes across the floor from the few tables of students who remain, slouched over their home fries and coffee (they drink coffee!). I have waited until the rush died down to sneak in for Sunday breakfast, not wanting to face the mobs alone. No one seems in a hurry, no one seems late for church. They seem sleepily content and utterly at home among the exposed brick and themselves. Why are all the white kids sitting together in the cafeteria?

"I'm not dressed right, though."

Janine scans the brown corduroy pants and itchy crew- neck sweater I purchased back in Memphis in a desperate, ill-destined attempt to fit preppily in and shrugs. "You're fine. The church here isn't like a real church. You can wear whatever you want."

So I drain my glass and put away my tray and follow Janine across the impossibly-picturesque campus with its ivy-covered buildings and graceful, curving walks and maples turning a fiery red to the lovely, stone church. Inside it was beautiful, all polished glowing wood and stained-glass windows rising up above the pulpit. Far more grand than Uncle Elmo's storefront church and far more traditional than Temple.

We sat down (in chairs, not pews, which was weird) and somebody handed us a program (for church? Also weird) and the choir began to sing.

Back in Memphis the only thing besides daydreaming which made church even remotely bearable was the music.

I understand that there are people in the world who don't like black church music, people who can sit and listen to a full-throated gospel choir belting out a song and remain unmoved. Or worse, consider such music somehow unseemly or low. I understand there are people like that and as a funky kind of quasi-Christian I love them, of course, and accept them just as they are. Which is frozen. I mean, seriously: just dead inside.

The whole history of black people in America can be heard in gospel music: our sorrow and suffering, our confusion and anger, our hope and endurance and moments of triumph and grace. Some of the songs we sang on Sunday morning were not technically gospels but spirituals, those beautiful and sacred sorrow songs of mostly-unknown- authorship black folks created from the misery and oppression of slavery. There's a reason many of these songs start low and slow and build to an emotional release.

It wasn't until I was out of college and studying black American history on my own that I learned gospel music is essentially an outgrowth of those spirituals, spirituals carted North at the turn of the 20th century and mixed with the blues. Unlike the spirituals, most gospel songs have known composers, musicians such as Charles Tindley and Thomas Dorsey who recognized that combining the scared with the secular created a powerful and moving sound that could not miss. It was tough going for those guys at first; many traditional, upstanding black churches shunned gospel, labeling it "the devil's music." Nobody ever said black people couldn't be as tight-assed as anybody else.

Fortunately by the time I came around most black churches had embraced gospel music. No matter the message from the pulpit, no matter how much shame or fear or damnation was thundered down upon my head in the churches of my childhood the music always made me feel better. The music was always lifesaving and soul- affirming. The music was the only thing that saved me, or ever came close to getting me saved.

So the music at Exeter was, that first Sunday, not only a shock but a deep disappointment. And though I appreciated the sermon—not for whatever was said, which I don't remember, but for how calm, and rational and, praise God, brief it was, almost like being in a lecture hall rather than a church—even though I appreciated the sermon and the fact that an hour after we sat down we were walking out again, once I found out that church attendance was, in fact, not mandatory at Phillips Exeter I never went back.

But my junior year somebody started a gospel choir on campus. Though I couldn't carry a tune in a bucket I was asked to join and I did. I still remember the first song we sang, a song I did not actually know but immediately loved. It's called "Encourage My Soul" (or Courage, My Soul) and was, in fact, composed by Tindley in 1905:

O courage, my soul, and let us journey on.
For tho' the night is dark, it won't be very long.

145

O thanks be to God, the morning light appears,
And the storm is passing over, Hallelujah!

I remember hearing one of the girls who wanted to start the choir sing that song for the first time. Her name was Bonita, she reminded me a bit of my sister and she had a strong, confident voice. If only for the space of the moment that she first opened her mouth and sang that song as we huddled together in the Afro-Exonian Society room, on the ground floor of the student center in the middle of that white and daunting place, I figured I might just be okay.

**

Blue Hill Avenue runs through the heart of black Boston, stretching from historic Roxbury down past Franklin Park and into the heavily-immigrant (Haitian, etc) neighborhoods of Mattapan. Blue Hill Avenue is lined with churches: churches and liquor stores and barber shops and hair salons and tiny, storefront restaurants and crappy dollar stores. No Trader Joe's or Target-like retailers or decent supermarkets. No substantial bookstores or thriving literary non-profits offering readings and classes and culture to the community but plenty of churches, churches galore. A riot of faith.

I have never counted all the churches lining Blue Hill Avenue but even standing in Mattapan Square and swiveling my head I can see three:

one Catholic, one Episcopal and one huge, evangelical, non-denominational one that clogs the avenue with cars on Sunday morn. I know that just out of eyesight are at least three more: a small, storefront church, a Baptist congregation, a repurposed synagogue.

It's not hard to make the argument that black people spend too much money on churches, to suggest that if we pooled our money and invested in land or profit-making businesses we'd be better off economically. Black Americans are easily the most religious, most-churched people in the country. According to the Pew Forum almost eighty percent of us say religion is very important in our lives (compared with 56% among all U.S. adults) and even most of us who say we're not affiliated with any particular faith say religion plays an important role in our lives. More than fifty percent of us claim to attend services at least once a week (I'm skeptical of this number) and nearly 75 percent of us pray every day. Ninety percent of us are absolutely certain that God exists.

What's more, black Americans give 25 percent more of their discretionary income to charity than do white Americans, and nine out of ten dollars we give goes to churches or other religious organizations. At the same time, African Americans remain, as a whole, at the bottom of the economic ladder, success stories aside.

Even a person who doesn't view faith as a kind of spiritual quid pro quo and God as a giant vending machine— drop some prayers in the slot, push the button and take out what you want—can wonder if something isn't off in this equation. Even a person not ready to toss out the baby of faith with the very dirty bathwater of Christianity's complicity in the wholesale purchase, resale, rape and oppression of African people in the new world can wonder if we shouldn't be a wee bit more discerning about this thing. Even a woman who considers the tenants of the so-called Prosperity Gospel anathema to the teachings of Jesus, can wonder: do you really believe God expects you to stay broke in this life? And if not, do you really believe She expects you to make some glitzy megaminister megarich because he tells you God doesn't expect you to stay broke in this life? Does that even make sense?

But, hey, I don't know. Black folks also spent something like 1500 billion on hair care and personal grooming products in 2009. So maybe pouring resources into our churches isn't the worst thing we could do with our money. Maybe the spiritual sustenance and nurturing we get in return is worth at least as much as a weave.

More importantly, maybe we would not have survived the brutal Middle Passage and slavery itself and rape and murder and lynching and Jim Crow and the whole myth of inferiority without some unshakable belief in a higher order of justice, salvation and ultimate love. The

Africans transported across the cold, gray Atlantic were not Christians, of course. What they did was take a Christianity meant to enslave them and twist it into something uniquely their own. Imperfect, sustaining and ultimately liberating.

Quibble, maybe. But I cannot argue with that.

**

I am thirty-nine and contemplating the contemplation of suicide. It is winter, early January, bleakly gray and bitter cold. The holidays, which I hate, are thankfully over but the stain of the expectations and forced frivolity and stuffed-in-the-closet aching loneliness linger along. I am somehow living in a city I do not like in a region to which I swore I would never return and it is winter, a season I fail to understand. Be careful what you wish for and what you swear against. There is snow on the ground, lots and lots of snow.

The dog needs walking, so I bundle myself and lace up my boots. I have two hours of relative freedom while the girl is in kindergarten and the baby is away at home daycare, a rambling, slightly dingy place where the children seem happy and fine and the stringy-haired, bespectacled, hippie-looking white woman seems loving and qualified but the smell is always slightly sour and the light a little dim and you just don't know. You just don't know.

But I need the time. Technically to write; I am supposed to be writing, to be finishing my third novel, my agent says come-on-come-on-come-on-you-are-already- behind-and-losing-readership-and-you-really-have- none-to-spare. So I need the time, technically to write in peace without little fists banging and little voices crying and little feet stumbling down stairs and damaging themselves, but, really, also just to have some breathing room from the demands of it all. Just to have a little peace.

But the dog needs walking. I trudge with her out into the snow. A storm blew through two days ago, a bad one, and the sidewalks are lined with canyons of white. We make our way down toward the park, one block, another and another and then we hit a stretch of unshoveled walk, a long one, running before two large and expensive houses made of stone and other fine materials. The driveways of both houses are pristine, someone might have gone over them with a blowdryer and so are the walkways between driveway and house, but the sidewalks down in front are untouched.

The sight first makes me furious, then plunges me into despair. A world so relentlessly selfish, a world in which such people not only live but thrive—look at those cars! Look at those houses!—makes me want to burst into tears. I burst into tears. The other side of the street is sidewalk-less, a common occurrence in this delusional little suburb which clings to a 1950s Ozzie and Harriet dream of itself, so I have to step into the street to navigate the section and I wonder what it would feel like to think about going ahead and lying down.

I don't think about lying down in the street, mind you. I think about thinking about lying down in the street. Back at home I stomp the snow from my boots just inside my front door and scramble for a towel to put them on so as not to leave a pool of wetness on the floor. I think about what it would be like, what it would feel like, to think about going into the kitchen and turning on the gas in the stove and going to sleep. Would it feel frightening to think those thoughts? Exciting? A great, swooshing relief? For the rest of my time alone I contemplate the contemplation of suicide. This is both further than I have ever come before and as far as I will allow myself to go, because of the children. I would never do it, because of the children. I never would.

**

"You want to go to church?"

I stand over the bed, looking down at my boyfriend, M. It is Sunday morning, around 8 o'clock in our Philadelphia apartment and something had pulled me out of bed, something that's been pulling at me for years but which I have successfully resisted until now. If I needed a word for this feeling I might label it guearning or yilt: equal parts a long-simmering yearning for the aspects of a church I loved in childhood (community, music, transportation outside of oneself temporarily, and, yes, love) and plain, old-fashioned guilt about not attending, about squandering God's day in laziness and decadence.

I am twenty-seven and in the nine years since Exeter I have probably been inside a church fewer than two dozen times, mostly for Christmas Eve or Easter service, or in service of a story while pursuing my career as a journalist. For some reason white editors loved to send me into churches in search of stories. Don't ask.

Still, I always missed it. Sunday mornings were fine, Sunday mornings lying in bed way past the time I should have been up, then rising for a leisurely brunch over the newspaper with or without the man in my life. Sunday mornings were fine when I didn't do go to church. But Sunday afternoons were terrible. Sunday afternoons sucked.

Sunday afternoon is the most melancholy part of the week, anyway. Sunday afternoon is like calendarized, existential despair. The weekend is over, the buzz has worn off, the man you wanted to love you has up and gone home. The workweek looms, you haven't done half of what you wanted or needed to do to catch up from the previous week and more is about to pile on. The light is fading, time is passing, you sit in your living room with the laundry piled in a basket before you and the dog hair you didn't vacuum and know in your heart it's another week closer to the grave and there's no Saturday night party or dinner or movie date or weeknight ritual to distract you from that fact, or the fact of our own essential aloneness in the world. Sunday afternoons are terrible. Or maybe that's just me.

But I had noticed that on the rare Sunday morning I got up and went to church Sunday afternoons were not so bad. I didn't feel so lonely, so essentially alone.

Also, now that I was out of the South and out of childhood (nearly twenty-eight) and had seen the world a little bit I'd come to realize that the church of my childhood was not the only possibility. There were other churches, other denominations, even other religions that I might consider. Sure, I'd probably go to hell for veering away from the straight and narrow path, the true path to salvation, but, by most accounts, that fate was already sealed. I might as well see if I could ease my Sunday afternoon loneliness.

Also: M had proposed. I, astonished and astonishingly, had accepted and we were scheduled to marry in less than a year. And there was no question: I wanted to be married in a church. But only the worst sort of hypocrite seeks a church wedding with no real interest/commitment/involvement in the church beyond that one day. I didn't want to be a hypocrite. I didn't want my family to come for my wedding and have the pastor mispronounce my name.

"Can't you go without me today?" M said, turning over and pulling the pillow over his head.

M was another issue. His family had vaguely attended some vague Presbyterian church when he was a child but they were in no ways religious and he had in no ways any guilt about/yearning for church. He was, however, willing to support my stumbling journey back to spiritual wholeness. As long as he didn't have to get out of bed early.

Also, M was white. This both was and was not an issue for me. Depending.

It wasn't an issue when we were alone, not back in those early days, though later it would become more of one. (This would not be his fault; the change would not be in M but in me, in my growing awareness of, and impatience with, the things he could know and not know, the things he could pay attention to and not pay attention to, the way what James Baldwin called a *willful innocence* could work in his life but not in mine.)

It wasn't a major issue when we were among M's family, or his friends and grad school colleagues. Most of these people were white, educated, liberal and either indifferent to my non-psychology, non-PhD self (which I preferred) or quietly titillated at the idea of being my friend. They loved me, or at least the idea of me.

It was a slight issue among my friends, most of whom were black but all of whom were well and truly accustomed to white people, having had to be. My friends accepted me and whoever I wanted to love, though once or twice a black acquaintance or co-worker would work up the nerve to voice disapproval of my private life ("What you doing with that white boy? Don't you have any pride?"). Quite often this was a man. Quite often he was either a player or a guy who himself dated only the brightest, lightest black women with the finest, limpest hair he could find.

But though M and I had been dating off and on for years by the time we moved to Philadelphia, I didn't know whether taking him to a black church would be an issue or not. Would he be comfortable? Would he make himself that way? Would the congregation accept him? Would they secretly roll their eyes, wondering what in the world had made me drag a white person up into the only place of sanctuary they had each week?

I had been to enough black churches in my life to know that one or two grains of rice in the coffee can was not unusual, especially not in the South. Black people have always been, by force, more accommodating of the wide range of human skin color created by four hundred years of

African and European mingling (forced and voluntary) than white people. But I also knew that with M in tow I'd be startling visible. There would be no sneaking into a sanctuary on Sunday morning and sitting in a pew toward the rear and letting the service wash over me to see if the water was warm or scalding hot. Whenever we went anywhere in the black world M outed me as the foreign spy I sometimes felt I was among my own people. This, of course, was my own problem and not his. But there you are.

So we started with the white churches. We started, in fact, with the whitest church I could find: the Unitarians.

I don't remember exactly which Unitarian Universalist church in Philly we went to; there are several. I do remember it as massive and imposing, a limestone castle rising up from the dirt, spires reaching toward the sky. I remember climbing tall steps to reach the front doorway and entering a sanctuary that seemed as vast and cool as the caves of Waitomo. I remember all of the people being white, though if the church were in Germantown or Mt. Airy where we lived this seems unlikely, a trick of the mind. I remember the self-conscious absence of anything resembling a Christian symbol: no crosses hanging over the pulpit or pictures of a glossy, blonde Jesus in the stained glass. I remember that the minute the music began I knew I would not be joining

that congregation, and that by the time the minister began his lecture—
for that's what it felt like, I wondered if I was supposed to take notes—I
was already done. I remember that everyone was very polite and kind as
we made our escape. I remember that at least it was short. And now I
know Unitarians take the summer off—the whole summer off from God!

We tried a few more white churches, Presbyterian (yawn) and white
Baptists (yikes) and another Unitarian (the same). We did not, of course,
try any Catholic churches; Catholicism had long been a vast, dark
mystery to me. It wasn't until college that I even met a black Catholic
person; before then I kind of assumed we were not allowed. Then I went
once with a friend to mass and realized that, in fact, I *wasn't* allowed -
not because of the color of my skin but because I hadn't been properly
sanctioned by whatever complicated hierarchy of men (men!) I could not
understand. When she stood up to go to receive communion I stood with
her, but she told me to sit back down. That was the last time I went to
mass.

Finally we stumbled somehow into a big, beautiful stone church on
Germantown Avenue. It was called the First United Methodist Church of
Germantown, and though we could see from the people flowing in one
Sunday morning that the congregation was predominantly white, we
could also see a fair number of black folks and other people of color

going in. And even other interracial couples (though, of course, they were all black men/ white women.) We went inside and everyone was friendly without being too friendly and we sat down and the choir sang, first a hymn and then a gospel song and then another hymn and then another gospel song, and then the minister, whose name was Theodore Loder, rose up in the pulpit and preached, not the fire-and-brimstone screeching of my childhood but not the monotone lecture of the Unitarians either (sorry), but something in-between, something impassioned and anointed and thoughtful and reasoned and I leaned over to M and whispered, "Bingo-"

A church requiring I leave neither my heart nor my head at the door.

**

Two of my siblings remain faithful and observant practitioners of an evangelical faith. The other two wouldn't know a church if it fell on them. As with most aspects of my life, I step somewhere in the middle. How this keeps happening I do not know.

Of all the non-church friends I have in Boston, which is to say the people I know from places other than my church, virtually none practice a religious faith or hold a belief in God. None of the men I've dated since the divorce were believers at all. Some of them, upon learning that I regularly attend church, looked at me as if they'd stumbled upon a caveman out in the backyard, squatting in the dirt.

This is especially true of the white guys. Black men, even if they do not attend church or believe in God tend to have enough home-training not to be openly disdainful of another person's religious beliefs. This is also more true of my non-believing white colleagues and friends than my black unbelieving ones. My sweet young students can be especially egregious in this regard; flush with the certainty and arrogance and discovery of youth they seize on any mention of God or religion or faith in some slave narrative were reading or some novel by Graham Greene and go at it with hacksaws, roaring disdain. *Was Phillis Wheatley on crack? Was David Walker an idiot? Harriet Jacobs, Frederick Douglass, Martin Luther King! All these people professing a belief not only in God in general but in a Christian God, the very same which the slave owners used to justify slavery! Sheesh! It's a wonder these people managed to not only endure but survive three hundred years of brutal oppression, create one of the most vibrant and influential cultures the world has ever seen and ineffably shape the American experience!*

Sigh.

Whenever some smug nonbeliever finds out I attend church and roars back in preparation for a lecture on my ignorance I hold up my hand: I'm not interested in persuasion or conversion. I don't care what other people believe or disbelieve or what impact it has upon their soul, all of which makes me a terrible Christian but there you *go.*

I'm also not interested in defending my beliefs, whatever they are, and especially not to people who consider it sport to belittle and mock faith or those who have it. Blind, arrogant atheism is just as tedious and dull as blind, arrogant faith. Whenever I encounter some smug atheist, someone desperate to lay out the Bible's inconsistencies and historical inaccuracies as if I have never considered them before, or point out the anthropological evidence against creationism, or patiently explain how faith is for the simple and weak-minded and religion is the masses' opiate (unlike, say, professional sports) I mostly want to yawn.

There was a book I read once, long ago. In fact the very story of how I found this book is one of those leaf-smacking moments of my life. I was at *The New York Times.* About *The New York Times* let me just say this: backstabbing, venomous, soul-crushing place to work. Yeah. Miserable place.

One day, wandering through the newsroom like a ghost, I came upon the table where the book reviewers would dump their load of review books for people to pick through and take home. A book leapt out at me, a book called *A Handbook for Constructive Living.* By some guy named

David K. Reynolds, PhD.

What made me pick up this book I do not know. It wasn't the title: I hated self-help books then and I hate them now and rarely am drawn to pick one up. It wasn't the cover; review copies of books are usually sent out with plain paper covers with only the title and author printed in chunky, block letters on front.

Regardless: I took it home. I opened it. I began to read and it was like a pillow coming off my face.

In the very first chapter Reynolds suggests this exercise: set a timer, find a focal point in the room - a picture, a vase, a chair—and stare at it. Keep your eyes and your mind on the object for three minutes, no more and no less. What you'll likely find, he writes, is that it's easier to keep your eyes focused on the object than your mind. That's because we have the most control over our actions and far less control over our thoughts— and almost no control over our feelings, at all. This is the problem with a feeling-centered life, a life in which actions and decisions and even thoughts are directed by how one feels. Why then build your life around the very aspect over which you have the least control?

This was a revelation.

Since at the time I was feeling miserable, terrified and stuck, this came as a swamping relief. Just because I *felt* terrified and desperate and unable to move ahead didn't mean I had to *act* that way! I didn't have to undergo years of therapy to figure out why I was miserable, or try to fix my feelings in some complicated and abstract way! I could simply acknowledge what I was feeling, see if those feelings offered any useful information (like: you need to flee the *New York Times)* and then do whatever needed to be done.

Know your purpose, accept reality and do what needs to be done.

Some people will say, "Yeah well, that's great but finding that book at just that moment was simply coincidence."

Others will say, "You manifested it. You needed an answer and so you looked around until you found one that fit."

I say: fine. Whatever. I choose to see God.

The book also explained the stages of development in Morita Therapy, a Japanese system upon which Constructive Living is partially based. Reynolds writes that from a Morita perspective, the most pitiful person in the world is one who is miserable, whose room is messy, and because he's so focused on his misery he doesn't notice the mess. He is to be pitied not because he's miserable; everyone is miserable sometime. He is to be pitied because his room is messy and he doesn't notice it. His life is happening and he's too busy wallowing in misery to notice it.

One step up (or one room; sometimes I think of it as a kind of transparent apartment building, floor upon floor) is a miserable man whose room is messy and he notices it is messy but this noticing only makes him more miserable. He wallows in the misery. Above him is a man who is miserable, he notices the messy room and though he is miserable he begins to clean it up. When asked why, he responds that he has learned he can distract himself from feeling miserable by cleaning— which is all well and good, but still a feeling-centered life. Above him a man cleans up his messy room but when asked why responds it is because the room needs cleaning. He is simply doing what needs to be done. And on and on and on, through several more layers of development and understanding that grow increasingly subtle, both simple and complex.

Something about this metaphor for layers of understanding and consciousness speaks to me. I can apply it to all kinds of things, from my own stumbling toward faith to an understanding of the way various privileges operate in the world to the existence of black Republicans.

In terms of faith, I envision that the first level holds those unquestioning inheritors of religious dogma that atheists so like to disdain. The mess in which they sit is not faith per se but the narrow, danger-making belief that theirs is the only path and that anyone choosing another is doomed to death, in either this world or the world to come. They aren't miserable (the stronger the faith the happier the person, in general) but they can make others that way. Also, yes, the world.

Above them by a step sit the hardcore atheists. They sit in rooms strewn with arrogance and condescension, stomping their feet on the floor in an attempt to step on the simple faith of the people below them. They're generally unhappier than the people below but at least they're looking down their noses at someone. They never look up.

I am forty six and for the first time in my life I consider the actual mechanics of ending my life. I stand in my kitchen and stare at the pile of dishes in the dish drain, and the crappy counters that won't get clean no matter how hard I scrub and the cabinets that need to be replaced. It's a Saturday afternoon in December, the holidays bearing down. The children are with their father; that relationship is intact and strong and given my family history its existence feels like one, small success in a string of failures on my part. And, yes, part of me knows there haven't really been a string of failures, or at least no longer a string than anyone else. Still, that's how it feels. I stand in the kitchen with my arms crossed tight, holding myself and considering.

There are two doorways, one to the hallway, the other to the dining room; they'd need to be covered up somehow, to keep the gas from spilling all over the house. Not, of course, that if I were going to actually do it, which I would not, I would do it while the children were here. Never. Still, even in idle contemplation, no sense blowing up the place.

I open my oven door and peek inside. It occurs to me that I don't know where the pilot light is. It's not like this oven is fancy, maybe $500 at Sears ten years ago. But it is fancier than the one I grew up with, with the little hole you had to stick a match into every time you turned it on. This oven self-lights, which means I'd have to find the pilot light and blow it out or risk baking my head. Which would be painful, if I were going to do it. Which I am not, of course, but if I were I'm just saying: I definitely would not want pain. I close the oven and go back to the living room.

I do not believe suicide is necessarily selfish, but I know my responsibilities. On bad days, and there are neither more nor less of them, I think the only reason to stay alive is for my children. This is reason enough, of course, but also sad. And impermanent; kids won't always be kids. My mother knows that.

What's interesting is that before motherhood, when taking my own life would have saddened a few people but devastated none, I never allowed myself to come as close to considering the deed as I have post-partum. Certainly there were days and evenings spent curled on the floor in despair, wondering how the hell to go and why. Certainly there were times when the idea of not being alive anymore seemed not frightening but comforting, a kind of restful sleep, but thinking about not being alive is not the same as thinking about being dead. And thinking about being dead is not the same as thinking about killing yourself. I never allowed myself to think about killing myself before I had children. Which is interesting.

Maybe this means I was never technically, clinically depressed, or maybe it means that deep down inside and despite myself I'm one of those Strong Black Women, TM who trudges stubbornly on despite everything. Or maybe it just means there really is a God.

Get pregnant.

What? Who me?

Get pregnant. You want to get pregnant.

Really? Then why am I twenty-eight, married and never considered it? Never gush at babies, hand people back their kids ASAR Why is even my husband surprised when I suggest it? My family too?

Yeah, yeah, yeah—just get pregnant. Then do it again. Trust me on this.

*

When my marriage was crumbling M and I clawed our way through a series of counselors, trying to hold on to the drifting pieces for the sake of the children if not for our own. One of the therapists, at the start of the first session, asked a question, a question she said had to be answered before anything else: "Do you want this to work? Do you want this relationship saved?" It was a terrible, necessary question and I had to tell the truth in answering it: "I *want* to want it to work, desperately. But not more than that."

I don't have to want to want to have faith; I've always wanted it. Even during the most rebellious or cynical times of my life, the times of greatest distance from the church of my youth or the church yet to come I still longed for faith the size of a grain of mustard seed. I still wanted it, not for what it could get me in this world or the next, but for the peace I knew—*I know*—it could bring. The peace I've witnessed on the faces and in the spirits and the lives of too many grounded, terrific and thoughtful people I've known to be discounted. The peace I've felt in precious, fleeting moments myself

**

A guy I once dated liked to say, "There are two kinds of people in the world: ones who do X and ones who do Y." This was his way of categorizing those who did not agree with him on any issue: people who thought The Three Stooges were geniuses and people who didn't. People who saw the special beauty of Formula One racing and those who could not. People who thought Rhode Island was the center of the universe and the misguided dopes who thought otherwise.

I didn't realize how deeply this division-process ran until one morning as we stood together in his kitchen making toast. "Do you have any peanut butter?" I asked, staring into the fridge.

"Why are you looking there? It's in the cabinet."

"Oh." I closed the fridge, moved across the room. "I keep mine in the fridge."

His coffee mug paused mid-air. "You what?"

"I keep my peanut butter in the fridge."

His face twisted in shock and disbelief. "Who keeps their peanut butter in the fridge?"

"Um, some people?"

He had never heard of such a thing, and even having heard it could not conceive of it. I might have admitted a preference for the sweet taste of roasted toddler toes for all his shock and disgust. "I guess there are two kinds of people in the world," I said, smiling desperately. I was in love with him and I could feel his so-called love for me slipping away but I didn't know why. "People who keep their peanut butter in the cabinet and people who keep it in the fridge."

"Nobody keeps it in the fridge," he said. "Nobody but you."

A few weeks later he dumped me, via email.

Looking back I can see what I should have said that night as we sat in his beautiful kitchen, discussing peanut butter: there are two kinds of people in the world. People who understand that the way they think and feel and perceive the world, their "system of reality," is neither universal nor inherently good or true, and people who do not. That's what I should have said, though he would not have heard me. Anyway, I was still too busy pretending I was in love with him and he in love with me.

So here's this about depression: There are two kinds of people in the world: people who get depressed, seriously, deeply depressed, and people who do not. People who know what it's like to submerge into despair, to feel the waves rise up over your head and smash you into the sand and people who get blue sometimes and get over it.

People who understand the urge toward suicide and people who do not. People who understand the urge to suicide so keenly they cannot imagine people who get through their lives never feeling the tug. Who know it as a yearning for release, an urge to just crawl up into your bed with your shoes on and close your eyes. People like that and people who have never, even in their darkest moments, considered it, for whom suicide is plainly, selfishly wrong. It's true: suicide is surely selfish. As selfish as demanding someone's continued presence, pain unaddressed. As selfish as love.

"I'm really struggling here," I tell a friend.

"Oh, you're fine."

"No, I'm not."

"Yes, you are. You're fine. You're beautiful and smart and talented, so what could be the problem? You're a little lonely and sad but you're fine."

Um, sure. Okay. Fine.

Sometimes a suicide attempt is a cry for help. Sometimes a suicide attempt is more like a scream, a pounding on the door, a table hurled across the living room. An exclamation point where previously has stood a period, unacknowledged, skipped right on past. *Excuse me, please, this hurts. This hurts, this hurts, I hurt, okay ? !*

My friend tells me I'm fine, fine, fine and I nod and smile and go home and look at the suicide note I have stored on my computer. It reads, "I told y'all I was tired."

I know this is terrible, but reading it makes me laugh.

**

The two most moving words in the Bible are these: "Fear not."

If you read the Bible (and I haven't, not really, not as much as I should) you'll hear these words spoken over and over again. In the Old Testament and the New Testament, in Isaiah and Deuteronomy, in Proverbs and the Psalms, in Matthew and Luke. It's what the angel said to Mary when delivering the news of her selection and what the angels said to the shepherds keeping watch over their flocks by night. It's what Jesus tells the disciples when he's coming to them across the waves and they freak out. "Be of good cheer, it is I. Be not afraid."

So much of human life, so much of human misery situates in fear. We are terrified, all of us, nearly all the time. Afraid of one another and of ourselves. Afraid of being hurt, of being abandoned, of being wounded. Of not having enough or filling a hole. Of growing up and growing old and most of all of dying.

"Be of good cheer, it is I. Be not afraid."

I am never afraid in my church. Never fearful, never lonely, never overwhelmed. I am sometimes sad—there is always sadness in a black church, which is one of the things I love, this courage to allow for the range of human emotions, to allow folks out from behind the suffocating mask. I am sometimes sad but I never despair. Standing in the congregation, lifting my voice with those around me, lifting our collective voice I experience a spirit and presence I can only call Divine. One part love, one part joy, one part peace, one part sorrowful recognition of the pain of the world and the possibility of transforming that pain. The older I get the less I care whether this Divine is human-caused or not, supernatural or energy manifest. I feel it, I know it, it's real and the weeks I am able to carry its light with me out the doors of the church and into my house and into my classroom and into the world are good weeks, glowing weeks, healthy weeks, weeks of building blocks. I only pray it might be so all the time.

"Fear not; for I am with you: be not dismayed; for I am your God: I will strengthen you; yea, I will help you; yea, I will uphold you with the right hand of my righteousness" (Isaiah 41:10).

I am never afraid in my church, and I am never depressed. I can't live there all the time, of course, and I know that even if I could it wouldn't be the same. Still, of a Sunday, it's enough.

**

In the end then, two things brought me fully and completely back to the church: depression and my children. Train up a child and you get the children too.

M and I moved to Boston when the children were three and two months old. I wasn't working, having mustered the courage to crawl out of the viper pit of *The New York Times* and focus on writing fiction full-time. We were in Boston because it was cheaper than New York and we could afford a house and because M had family here who might help with the children, all of which was wonder- fill, but Boston had never been my favorite town. I had no friends or my own family, had very few connections among black people, in general. I was lonely and sleep-deprived and out of sorts. And I wanted my children to have a religious foundation, a system of belief (which they could later rebel against; hey, if you don't give them something they'll find it and it will be you), a church home, a church family, a community, love. Love, love, love.

One thing I knew, however, as I began visiting churches in this strange, new city was that I would not be returning to the church of my youth. I did not want my children to grow up with a thundering God of condemnation and fear. I wanted a progressive faith community, one in which the Word was not used to separate and divide but to extend and include.

No litanies of sin from the pulpit, no constant roll call of the saved and the damned. No financial requirements involving buying one's pew or one's way into heaven by lining the pastor's silk purse. No "Touch not my anointed" elevation of the pastor as being holier-than-us and no Prosperity Gospel nonsense, either. If the Jesus of the Bible approves this vision of a materialistic, bling-flinging, vending machine God I will eat my hat when I get to heaven. If there is a heaven. I don't claim to know.

Most of all, no using of God's word to condemn any group of human beings because of the color of their skin or the shape of their genitals or the denomination of their church or the name of their God or who they loved or, really, anything except possibly their loud and insistent belief that they possessed the right to stand for God and condemn. Specifically, no hating on homosexuals.

Which was a problem, because the other big thing I wanted from a church was that it be black. I wanted, even needed, a black church home for myself, and I wanted one for my children. I wanted them to grow up in a church firmly rooted in the black church tradition (regardless of the actual color of the congregants), wanted them to know that whatever its faults and shortcomings and blind spots and flat-out wrongs the black church is beautiful and powerful and capable of sustenance.

I wanted my children to know the history of the black church, all of it, good and bad. I wanted them to know that whatever its problems we, as a people, a forced creation of Africa and America, would not have survived without a strong and abiding faith in community and in God. And yes, a Christian God, the God of the slave traders and the slave owners and the founding fathers, a Christian God, for that's what we were left with, a single, unifying God who pulled us together from many people and many ethnic groups and made us one. And a church that served as sanctuary and spark. Civil Rights Movement? Hello?

I also hoped for a community of stable, loving, successful and grounded black folks in which to submerse my children. Even though their father and I sought out a diverse preschool and chose, among the four elementary schools in our predominantly-white town, the one in which the population of white children fell below 90 percent (another story) I knew the simple truth was that my children would grow up mostly surrounded by white people. Which was fine; but I wanted to find for them, if I could, an extended black family to stand in for mine, which was three thousand miles away. I wanted a church full of black grandparents and aunts and uncles. I wanted both my son and my daughter to know, firsthand and up close, strong, loving, stable black men (my brother definitely counts, but it's hard to make an impression on kids you see only twice a year).

So: a socially progressive, non-condemning, community-active, gay-welcoming black church. Right.

The good news is this: nothing's too hard for God. After six months of randomly visiting churches it occurred to me to get on the internet instead of the street and do some research. Two or three clicks through a Google list (I wish I could remember the keywords I used) and I found it: Union United Methodist Church in Boston's South End neighborhood.

I discovered that just months before this predominantly African-American but racially diverse church had become a reconciliation congregation. That means we "affirm the full participation in all aspects of our church life of all who confess Jesus Christ as Lord and Savior, regardless of their race, color, physical challenge, sexual orientation and/or affectional orientation."

That Sunday I got in my car and drove across town to see this thing for myself.

"Welcome to Union!" said the greeter at the door.

She was a beautiful older black woman, stately and thin and elegant in her blue suit and matching heels, her silver hair swinging around her face like a curtain. As I was thanking her I noticed her eyes go over my shoulder and her face, already smiling, light up even more. Walking away, I glanced back to see who she was so delighted to see. It was two white men, impeccably dressed and obviously a couple. She hugged them both; they hugged her back.

Ten minutes later, when the choir marched in singing I knew I was home.

**

My friend Edie has the best metaphor for the Divine I've ever heard. My friend Edie is actually older than my mother and also white and married and by any normal course of events we would never be friends. But we are, having met through our church. Not just our church, but a woman's group I was somehow moved to try to start when I first joined (and this in itself is a miracle, because I am no starter or even joiner of groups. Somebody's hand was in this.)

EDIE's CREDO:

1. The word God has become freighted down with too many meanings, so when it is used now, it no longer brings to mind the unfathomable mysteriousness we are trying to express. I am trying to refer to God as X and consider my quest "Solving for X!" Seriously, try putting X in place of God in your thoughts and prayers and see how refreshing that is.

2.   I think X is totally right brain and totally left brain. That's why those statements about tragedy. (I had complained to her about people attributing hurricanes, earthquakes and the Japanese nuclear disaster to the will of God): you know deep down that both sides of your brain are necessary in order to grasp X. If you have to ignore one side, you are not seeing what X really is.

3.   I try not to be convinced of something by people who quote the Bible to prove a point. The God of the Hebrew Bible is enough to make your hair stand on end —talk about a nasty, vicious, abusive lover! (If

you really want to quote Scripture to justify what your heart tells you to do in terms of asking questions, look at Psalm 19: "I want to dwell in the house of the Lord all the days of my life—to behold the beauty of the Lord and to INQUIRE in his temple." How hypocritical of me to do something I have just advised against.)

4. Personally, I find the metaphor of my being a cell in the body of X to be helpful. I am essential to X at the same time I am not essential. My only leap of faith is that I do believe that X has meaning and that that meaning is good; I am unable to grasp that meaning yet, just as a cell in my lungs probably doesn't really grasp my brain cells' reality or function.

5. Jesus taught that there were two commandments: love X with all your heart and love your neighbor as yourself. Keeping these guideposts in mind helps me when I get bogged down in too much verbiage.

6. Others' paths to understanding are not necessarily my paths. Sometimes hearing about or seeing a faithful person's journey really helps, but it's still his or her path, not necessarily mine. I think of this sometimes in the Adult Classes when I hear this person or that speak. It is so clear they have found their paths and keep to them faithfully. I once thought I wanted to be like them, but that is not to be. They are cells in the liver and I am a cell in the lung. They are not "wrong" and I am not

"right" in a universal sense. They are perfectly what they should be.

7. I am only sure that X exists and that X is evident in love, laughter, music and light.

MY CREDO:

Everything Edie said.

I believe in God the Father. Also in God the Mother, because sometimes that Father stuff gets a little difficult. Also in God as Spirit, as Love Manifest, as the Collective Divine (as in Namaste, the divine in me acknowledges the divine in you) and as X. All of that, and more than I can articulate properly and some of it is conflicting and some of it is not.

I believe that this Divine X exists, that something bigger and more potent and more angled toward good than me or you or all of us exists, and that at moments in my life I felt this presence as tangibly as I feel this keyboard I'm typing on.

I believe in X and that Jesus was either the son of X or The Son of X, and to me it almost doesn't matter which one of these things is true. (I hope this doesn't get me kicked out of my legitimately Christian church. I love that place.) That the historical Jesus, the Jesus of the Bible spoke and acted from the power of some outrageous goodness and love seems clear to me. He was a man of great compassion for the poor and the persecuted, the unloved and the oppressed. He rejected the systems and powers of that oppression, and warned against the accumulation of money and wealth. He hung around with prostitutes and seemed, by all respects, not to consider women less worthy than men. He preached a mighty reconciliation, and that is powerful stuff.

For all the troubling things in the Bible I have yet to find anything attributed to Jesus I cannot get behind. In fact, much of what Jesus preached was downright radical, subverting not only both Jewish and Roman law but patriarchy, accepted social status and the rigid dogma of the time. Where did such courage and insight come from if not from God? Your mileage may vary, but I'm going with that.

More movingly, I find the idea of a God so full of love and perfect understanding, an X so mysterious and great that X even understands that it is this very Xness which keeps X ultimately separate from us. An X who understands it is that very Xness which renders X unable to fully grasp the one big thing: what it means to be human. So X becomes human. X allows X to feel pain and sorrow, fear and loneliness and, yes, despair, so that when you are lying among the dust and dog hair and insect carcasses on the floor beneath your desk one bitter, gray Sunday afternoon, sobbing and unwilling to go on, you can call on X and X will come and lie down with you. None of that carrying you across the sand business; X is right there in the dirt with you, also wounded, also sobbing. And you are not alone.

Which means that after a while you can get up out of there.

**

So, let's start again:

I am depressed. I hate even writing that, so I crawl beneath my desk and cry for a while. But after a while I claw my way up through the mud-grave of depression to level-ground, not to sunshine or blue skies or any of that crap but at least to air and I take the dog for another walk. This one around the neighborhood.

All of a sudden fall has arrived, seriously this time. The trees have burst into color, or died into it, everywhere is golden beautiful. I walk beneath a junk maple growing along the sidewalk and it showers me with small, yellow leaves. Without really trying I reach out my hand and grab one. It's small and curled and also sports a gaping hole; the moths have been busy this year. Still, a catch is a catch and luck is luck. I stuff it in my pocket, hole and all. Broken and imperfect and beautiful. The dog and I walk on.

V
MATCH POINTS

Love does not begin and end the way we seem to think it does. Love is a battle, love is a war, love is a growing up.
James Baldwin

For the life of me I cannot remember the date of my divorce.

It would be easy enough to look it up; three steps to the file cabinet, a few rifles through the mess. I have looked at that particular file only twice in the last six or seven years and only then because some procedure (refinancing, etc) demanded it, but still I find it curious that neither the day, the month or even the year is seared into my brain. I can remember my wedding day but then, of course, that's different.

I'm pretty sure it was December. Cold and dull outside, the sky the slate gray of winter and regret. There may or may not have been dirty snow on the ground but it wasn't snowing that morning. That much I would remember because I dislike driving in the snow. It would have been too much. For the same reason it must not have been too close to Christmas, because I hate Christmas and the irony of one of the most painful days of my life falling too close to that excruciating day of forced and false frivolity would have cemented things better. At least I think.

What little I remember comes in flashes: my surprise at the flat, featureless form of the courthouse, not a column or soaring buttress in sight. A hallway full of laughing white men in business suits. Wooden benches, worm smooth. I remember hoping I would not have to see M before the actual trial or meeting or whatever it was, and hoping that he would come alone, unaccompanied by the woman who would become his second wife, because I was alone. It had not occurred to me to ask anyone to come with me, and anyway, who would I ask?

I remember the courtroom itself was small and cheap looking and like nothing on television, though it strove for some dignity with walls I remember as deep maroon. I'd been in plenty of courts before but always as a journalist, a spectator, not involved. These were usually criminal courts, federal courts, rooms grand and imposing and large with the judge way back off from the gallery and up on high like some kind of god. This courtroom was small and close and claustrophobic; when the judge came in she didn't have to climb or step up to her bench, just walked over and sat down.

She was a woman; I remember that. Not black, maybe white, maybe Hispanic. Maybe Martian for all I knew or cared. She called our case and asked us some questions and we stood before her like criminals, necks bent, eyes down and when she began to lecture us about the need to cooperate as parents even if we had failed as husband and wife part of me expected the guards to come and drag me away.

Then she said something along the lines of, "I find on this date blah blah blah that the marriage of Kimberly and M, having reached a stage of irreconcilable repair, to be dissolved" and what was left of my heart crumbled to the floor. Then she said something along the lines of "I am sorry for the sake of A and G that you two were not able to make this marriage work," and the names of my children in this stranger's mouth made me want to vomit and then pick up a chair and smash her in the face. Who the hell was she anyway? What the hell did she know?

When she hit her gavel (or said "Case closed" or whatever the hell she did) I turned and got out of there, stumbling nearly blind down the stairs and out the door and to my car. I waited until I was out of the parking lot and on some side street in the surrounding suburb before I pulled over and sobbed my heart out. I don't remember where I was but I do remember, quite clearly, swearing to the skies:

Never again. Never again for this marriage thing. If for no other reason than never again would I give some stranger the right to sit in judgment of my heart.

**

Not that I'd been thinking about remarrying anyway.

I didn't get divorced thinking there was something better out there. I did not break up my family expecting to later slip down to the Man Mall and pick up Husband 2.0. I may not be the sharpest knife in the drawer but I'm far from delusional. I got divorced in order not to die, to not kill myself, having decided not to kill myself mostly for my children. I mean this quite literally.

I was forty years old and not hideous-looking when my marriage ended, but when I crawled out from the rubble of my twenty-year relationship I thought, "Well, that's the end of that."

That being the possibility of me ever having a loving, lasting relationship. I pretty much assumed that, like my mother and countless other black women I knew, I'd had my one and only chance and I'd screwed it up. To the back of the line! And the line has stopped!

It wasn't The Ex's fault. He was not to blame, at least no more so than anybody else. In fact, I was pretty sure the person to blame for the failure of my marriage was me. I read somewhere once that when a relationship tanks men think, "Boy, something was wrong with her" while women think, "Boy, something was wrong with me."This is a generalization but not much of one; not all women internalize blame but plenty of us do and so did I. Something was wrong with me, clearly. Since (a) the Ex was a good man, flawed and ill-fitted but well-intentioned, and (b) he said he loved me then clearly the only logical explanation for our inability to make things work was (c): I was one jacked-up human being. One broken appliance, one faulty, defective piece of human workmanship. That being true I could run around trying to find another electrical outlet to plug myself into, but what would be the point of that?

Then too, there was the simple math of the situation. Take the number of 40-50 something-year-old men in any given East Coast city. Subtract the married and the gay (and the married *and* gay). Subtract those who only date women fifteen to twenty years younger than themselves. Subtract those under five-foot-ten (I'm five-foot- ten and yes, it matters. I used to say under six feet but I've compromised. Give me a break.) Subtract the white men who won't date black women and the black men who won't date black women and what at first seemed like Lake Michigan if not an actual ocean has transformed into a puddle any toddler can skip across.

"Oh, you're so attractive and so smart and so accomplished and so lovely, you'll surely find someone quick," said some of my women friends. "Just live your life, you'll be surprised, love comes when you're not looking for it, the only problem you'll have is deciding whether you want to be bothered or not."They said all this and more but it should be pointed out that all of these kind and well-meaning friends were white and therefore really had no frickin idea what they were talking about. There are parallel universes for black women and white in America. They do not cross.

None of my black women friends said any such nonsense. Not V. or B. or B. or M. or J. or any of the other attractive, smart, accomplished, lonely and very single black women I know.

They said, "Girl, it's rough out here."

They said, "Come on out if you have to, but don't expect much."

They said, "Better make your peace with being alone."

So I tried to make my peace with it. I wasn't giddy at the prospect of being alone but I'd decided, made a very conscious choice to live with it. After misery, non-misery is plenty palatable. After hopelessness just being "eh" is pretty good. All I wanted was to be able to breathe again, not to suffocate. I crawled out from the rubble, picked the plaster from my hair. Attended the children. Cried. Got some therapy. Worried about the children. Practiced yoga. Checked on the kids. Cried some more.

Slowly, achingly, things settled down. The children stabilized, shaken but not destroyed. I got the job I needed and so it seemed, contrary to most predictions ("Divorce devastates women financially," warned one counselor we saw) the kids and I would still be able to eat and sleep indoors. I cried and stopped and exercised and stopped and went to therapy and stopped and went to church and stopped and went again and felt the anvil swinging over my head slowly roll away. I wasn't happy, but I was no longer miserable.

In other words, I was making my peace with the way things were.

Then arrived The Poet. Just plunged from the sky into my life like a meteorite. I don't know if love comes when you're not looking for it but I know that hope does. Which really sucks.

**

Here's a list of the men I have dated in the past six years, annotated and in the order, more or less, of their appearance in my life.

The Poet

The Social Worker

The Born-Again African/Black Nationalist The Spy

Steve, the Asshole Lawyer, He Who Shall Be Named

The Health Care Professional The Philosopher Bicyclist The Stalker The Best Gay Friend

The Cambridge Liberal The Writer, God Forbid

Those are the major characters. There were more: men with whom I corresponded or even met for coffee or a drink and never again. Like the bald, Libertarian filmmaker whose political philosophy mostly boiled down to smoking pot. Tall, landscaper who would not stop talking about himself. And the sad sack guy who slumped over his beer at the Ritz Carlton bar while telling me how his much-younger, second wife cheated and how hard it was raising a 4 year old in his fifties and how much he hated this dating. "I'm so tired of these endless job interviews," he said. "Are you interested or not?"

There was the sweating, socially-awkward guy in a Members Only jacket who texted me the next day to say that I was so beautiful and that it probably meant I wouldn't want to see him again. Sadly, he was correct. And the tightly-wound, narcissist pilot I met at Au Bon Pain in Brookline who got very defensive at having never been married (I didn't ask) and who discussed, also unasked, the most recent love-of-his-life: "I hated her. She was despicable. If she stepped in front of my car I wouldn't stop. Want to go out Saturday night?"

There was the telephone line technician from Framingham who I liked a lot and who, after our first meeting, wrote me an email saying, "I felt a strong chemistry between us. I don't remember the last time, I've enjoyed a conversation more, if ever. But we live too far apart." Framingham is twenty-two miles from Boston, maybe a forty-minute drive. This turned out to be a common element of the men I met online, a reluctance to search for love outside a two-mile radius of their couch. I guess I'm the wrong person to judge, since I was willing to go to Texas for the right person. Now I understand the appeal of the All-American Girl Next Door. She's next door.

There was the sweet 26-year-old kid who sent me an email saying I was "too cute to ignore." Naturally, I was flattered. But twenty-six? "Dude!" I said, "I have tee-shirts older than you!" (I stole that line.) When we met for coffee he tried to flirt and I tried to pretend the words coming out of his mouth didn't sound like toddler talk. Neither one of us succeeded. How men do it I have no idea. (Actually…)

There was also the guy I like to call *The Universe Laughs.* He came into my life, I guess, because at one point, as I was bemoaning my state of loneliness, my friend Jackie suggested I listen to the wisdom of Oprah and put out a request to the Universe.

"Write down what you want in a man," she said. "Be specific. Then put the list in a drawer somewhere and wait."

I'll be honest: this "Ask the Universe" stuff sounds to me like so much balderdash. Even if The Great Oprah Herself wrote it on a (donated) car and parked it in my driveway I'm not sure I could make myself believe that good things happen to people because they think they will and bad things—loneliness or divorce, war or famine or earthquake or tornadoes or childhood leukemia or being hit by a truck as you hiked on your way to work—happen because those poor suckers just failed to think positively enough. If that's really the way the universe works then the universe sucks. Seriously.

But Jackie is one of the smartest people I know and a good friend, so to humor her and distract myself I made a mental request of the Universe. I was too lazy to actually write it down but one morning as I sat swaying on the trolley as it rattled its way up Commonwealth Avenue I said to the Universe, "Okay. I would like a tall, black man, please."

Already you see the flaw.

After conducting my business at Boston University where I'd been headed, I jumped back on the trolley and headed back downtown. Near the Public Garden I emerged from the underworld and headed toward my class for the morning. Just as I was passing a tobacco shop at the edge of the Boston Common a tall, black man in a black polyester track suit came strolling out and fell into step beside me. Didn't even break stride.

"Hello!" he said. "You're beautiful. Can I walk with you?"

I started to laugh; he took this as a hopeful sign. He wore a Red Sox cap and blinding white sneakers and smoked a cigar and I could tell almost instantly from the huckster way he spoke and the pimp-swinging way he walked that we would never fit. By the time we got to the building where my class was held he'd learned my first name and I'd learned that he was still married ("But baby I'm free in my heart") currently unemployed ("I used to work up at the ballpark. Then some things happened and now I don't anymore.") and quite possibly on the wrong side of the law.

Hah hah, Universe.

Most of these guys, with the notable exception of Steve The Asshole Lawyer He Who Shall Be Named, were good and decent human beings. Most came to the connection with the best intentions he could muster, bringing all of his gifts to bear. So did I. And yet each of these connections failed.

Some failed gently, a raindrop upon a leaf. Some failed like the rainy season in West Africa: muddy, relentless, thunderously loud. Some were so obviously doomed from the start it's a wonder we even took the damn thing on. Sort of like Newt Gingrich's presidential campaign.

When you are forty years old, or forty-five, or fifty- one and a woman and facing the cool, hard reality of wanting to find a partner with whom to share the tattered remnants of your life and you work your way through a string of no-gos and you tell all your friends and they pile on the platitudes you can come to one of two possible conclusions:

Men are hopeless and real love itself impossible, a fairy tale told and believed only by fools. The sole real choice is between settling for a long, irritated life with the least-useless man you can find (or least until he cheats on or abuses or abandons you) or facing facts and staying resolutely alone.

Or:

Each failed connection is simply prelude, preparation for Mr. Right. If Mr. Right II seems to be taking his sweet time to come along it's simply because you are not ready for him yet, you are still dating yourself and healing your wounded heart and finding your center and learning whatever it is you have to learn from these people who come into your life because that's why they're there, of course, to teach you. You're just a slow learner is all. God/The Universe/Oprah has a plan. Things will work out, there's someone for everyone, a lid for every pot, it's always darkest just before the dawn and all you have to do is keep getting out there and living your life and love will come ambling along when you least expect it, sort of like an errant dog. One day you'll open up your front door and there it will sit, scratching itself.

We might, were we trying to frame the following events as a coherent narrative, call these the yin and yang of Dating In Midlife. One side hopeful and the other despairing, one rose-colored glasses and the other gimlet-eyed, one stance bitterly resigned and the other hopelessly, helplessly naive. We might depict these opposing stances as two little figures on each of my shoulders, one a red-cloaked devil dancing on my left, the other a beautiful, dreadlocked angel in white meditating on the right. We might set up the telling of this tale as a battle between these two forces, or journey from the dark into the light.

Or we might just tell the truth about how things went/ and see what comes of it.

"Relax," said a friend. "Love happens when you least expect it."

We sat at her kitchen table in the sunlight, her gigantic dog sleeping at our feet. Her home was cozy: warm and lived-in and comfortable. The linoleum on the floor was a dull yellow, the wall tiles a very Seventies pink but she was happy with her outdated kitchen and her husband and her life. We drank tea.

"What does that mean?" It had been two years since my divorce, maybe six months since the Poet and I was sad and lonely and hopeful and pissed off at the world for making me that way—mostly the hopeful part. If the universe was going to promise it had damn well better come through.

"Love is...serendipity."

I locked my eyes on my teacup to keep them from rolling from my head.

"You can't force it. That's the problem with online dating: it makes people believe they can just pick out a lover or a spouse from a catalog. It doesn't work that way."

"Did you ever try online dating?"

"Me?" She laughed. "No, not me. But I've seen the commercials."

"Right." I sipped my tea.

"All these people out there, desperately searching for the thing that cannot be tracked down. Love comes when you're not looking for it. "

I would hear this particular bit of wisdom many times in the years to come, but this was the first time. It startled me. I'd never heard such a thing before. Being married shields you from a lot of foolish ideas about finding love, just as having children shields you from a lot of foolish doggerel about childlessness, and being childless shields you from a lot of worthless utterings about having kids. Etc.

"So...don't seek and ye shall find?"

My friend nodded. "Something like that."

She's my friend so I didn't argue, just changed the subject. Still, every time I hear this fine of thinking (and I hear it a lot) I scratch my head. By this line of wisdom, it's the wanting of love that's the problem, not the lack of it. If there's no love in your life the problem is that you want it too much.

Does this work with other basic human needs? Should we say, don't go looking for water, water will come looking for you? Food is serendipity? The next time I walk across the Boston Common should I lean over that homeless guy's little cup and whisper sweetly, "Dude, shelter will come when you stop looking for it. Oh, you have? How's that working out?"

This is nonsense. Childish, romantic nonsense and balderdash, and it perfectly matches our nonsensical misunderstanding of love itself. We think love is some magical, mystical feeling over which we have no control, some wind sprite which blows into and out of our hearts by the whims of the gods. Love is visited upon us from the outside; we have no say in finding it or choosing it or keeping it, our role is to walk the earth blindly until we trip and fall into the hole of love and then just as easily trip and fall out. Our upbringings, our perceptions, our childhood wounds, the dictates of society that we internalize, our conscious and subconscious understandings of ourselves—all of these have nothing to do with the choosing of another human being with whom to invest our heart. No, that action takes place somewhere out there beyond us in the spirit world. You can't control who you love, or whether you will love at all.

What a dangerous, destructive and punitive belief.

Still. It's true enough that The Poet arrived when I wasn't looking for him. I didn't even want to attend the event at which we met.

I had finished classes for the day and had already schlepped home to run the afternoon gamut of child pickups and dropoffs and dinner prep etc when I got a call from the chairman of my department. He wanted to know if I would say a few words at the event that evening. It was a celebration of Langston Hughes and some poet was reading his work but they wanted someone to kick things off.

"Of course," I said. Though I had not been planning to attend, and though I now had to scramble for a sitter and rush back into the city by six.

"And you can join us for dinner afterward. We're taking The Poet out."

It sounded glamorous, not to mention a wise political move. But all I could think of was that going to dinner meant two more hours on the sitter's dime. I declined.

For the reading I didn't even bother to change whatever wrinkled clothes I had on, just snatched all the necessary pieces into place and got on the subway, writing my comments as we rattled along. My plan was to speak and sneak, slipping out at the earliest possible opportunity and when The Poet walked into the auditorium the plan did not change. He was black (I'd figured that much; the reason my presence was so desired) and tall and broad-shouldered but also big-eared and slightly dorky, as much Urkel as Denzel. I was not impressed.

Then he began to read.

"I want to start with a poem for my father," he said. "We lost him last year."

By the end of his first poem I was shredded. By the time he finished for good I was confetti, tossed into the air. He could have swept me up with his hands and dumped me in his pocket. He could have gathered me like lint.

I shoved aside at least three undergraduates to get to the chairman of my department, who was finalizing dinner plans on his cell phone.

"Um, think I'll join you after all."

Until The Poet I think I thought my choices among men were pretty black and white—as in I could either date a white man who might meet me educationally and intellectually but not culturally or I could date a black man who might meet me culturally but not in other ways. That's not to say I knew no intelligent, educated black men: I did. Most of them dated white women, or preferred sisters far more fair than I. This may seem a generalization but all I can tell you is that in three years at Exeter and four years at Duke, not one black man ever asked me out. Not one. I was going on what I knew.

Then here came the Poet: tall and fine and sharp as shit and a writer and reader and lover of literature (!) who could commiserate about Teaching While Black in a white institution but who'd also taught in prison and knew how to fight and could spend the morning talking smack at the barbershop. He had voice like Barry White. He called me "woman" and made me feel like it. And his poetry was beautiful: lyrical, vulnerable, courageous. Here was a man who paid attention to the world and to what it meant to be human inside of it. And he liked me. He really, really liked me, or so it seemed. Suddenly I believed. Suddenly it all made sense, suddenly my improbable and sometimes-painful path to that moment glittered with purpose. Suddenly all the romantic crap about destiny and soul mates and love finding you when you least expected it seemed real and possible. We were, without a doubt, *perfect* for one another. Just look at us.

You can see where this must lead.

That he lived and taught and wrote in a college town a thousand miles away was a nuisance but not insurmountable. That he was well over forty but had never been married seemed like a gift (no baggage for him! Less baggage for us!). That he spent most of our long, phone conversations talking about himself, and never, ever asked about or even acknowledged the existence of, my children seemed fine. He was interesting. I was interested! It would all work out just fine.

But after days of marathon phone sessions and two or three days of daily email he'd slip and fall off the face of the earth. Then days would pass without word from him, days and weeks until suddenly he'd somehow manage to get his fingernails back upon the surface of the planet and re-emerge.

"Long-distance relationships are hard," he explained. Turned out he'd just gotten out of one, in which one of them had moved finally to be with the other, only to have things fall apart.

"Hard but not impossible," I chirped. Suddenly I was Miss Optimism. Suddenly I was Little Suzy Can Do. I decided what we needed was a romantic weekend to seal the deal and so I made up an excuse to be in his college town. *I'm giving a reading!* Which was certainly plausible but let's just say it was a good thing he didn't care enough to check it out.

That evening he came to my hotel, asked how my reading had gone, took me to dinner. Afterwards we went back to the hotel and to bed.

It was terrible.

When it comes to love I can delude myself with the best of them. But not during sex.

In bed with a man I am both defenseless and hyperalert. In bed with a man I can tell if he loves me or not and if he loves me not and if I want him to love me my whole body rebels. Stomach clutches its middle. Heart crosses its scrawny little arms and says, "No." Gut shakes its head in disgust. "We don't like this. No, we don't."

I felt sick. I started crying. He patted my back like you pat a dog, a dog you are a little afraid of. Which made the crying worse.

"I'm sorry," I said, sniffling like a toddler. "Not very sexy, I know."

"It's human." Ever the Poet.

Then he got up and went home. The next morning I drove myself to the airport and flew back to Boston.

"His loss," said my friends. "Jerk. Asshole. Egomaniac."

Well, yeah. But it was my loss I was heartbroken about.

What I had lost was not just The Poet but the cool, insulating comfort of disbelief. What I had lost was not just the fantasy of the perfect man (for surely that's what it was, a fantasy) but the fantasy that I had somehow moved beyond the reach of desiring love. Suddenly I not only wanted to love and be loved again, but I **believed** it was possible. This was the start of nothing good.

Buddhists believe that desire is the root of all human suffering. It's not the not having of the things you want that makes it painful, it's the wanting itself. The Buddha, figuring this out, left his wife and children and kingdom and money and furniture and went out and sat beneath a bodhi tree until nothing much mattered anymore. After that he was fine.

Unfortunately, there are no bodhi trees in Boston. Just very rocky ground.

**

Dating in one's forties resembles dating in one's twenties the way the Tour de France resembles a Sunday afternoon ride in the park: only technically are the motions the same. One is just about a thousand times longer and harder and more uphill than the other. And in one somebody is probably going to get hurt.

It's not just the obvious things that make dating in midlife difficult. It's not just that most men capable of commitment and partnership are already partnered off, or that the addition of children greatly complicates everything. It's not simply that many men want women ten to fifteen years younger than themselves.

The bigger problem is that at forty self-delusion is like getting out of bed in the morning: a lot harder than it used to be. Love, romantic love, depends upon illusion, on smoke and mirrors, fairy dust and make believe. In the kingdom of romance, illusion is coin of the realm. Most people fall head over heels not with the person actually standing before them but with their own giddy projection, lit by kliegs, filmed in Technicolor, cast upon a human screen.

Falling in love is like falling off a mountain; everything around you becomes an impressionist blur. It's on' when you hit the ground and get down to the business of relationship that things snap into focus. By then you're married and have children and a mortgage and a dog and so when you look over at the person you thought was Denzel Washington mashed up with e.e. cummings and Bruce Lee and it turns out to be more like Bill O'Reilly mashed up with Barney Fife you're committed. Which is not to say stuck.

But at forty-five entering love is more like uphill hiking than falling. At that speed, you can see everything. Few people can stand up under that kind of scrutiny.

It was November when I abandoned all hope for The Poet. The holidays were lonely and miserable whenever the kids went off to celebrate with the Ex and his full and burgeoning family. Then came

January, which in Boston means cold, snow, misery, grayness and more cold. By the time February dragged around I knew I needed some diversion to pull me through the next few remaining months of a New England winter. It wasn't that I didn't know how, or was too afraid, to go to movies alone or out to dinner alone or take classes alone or stay home alone or otherwise "date myself"; it was that I was sick of that crap.

"Just live your life," friends advised.

"Don't focus on it! Then you'll meet the right one."

"Get out there in the world and mix it up."

Nice advice, only if I was any more out there in the world I'd be homeless. I was juggling three official jobs (teaching, writing and appearing regularly on a local television talk show) and a few more, unofficial ones (parent, driver, housekeeper, cook). I had so many things on my plate there wasn't room for a fork and I met plenty of people every month but most of them were women and the men were all either married or gay. You know the drill.

It was time to take matters into my own hands. It was time, I decided, to online date.

This was 2007, when online dating still contained a whiff of shame and desperation, when admitting out loud that you had signed up for a Match.com subscription was like admitting you ate mostly government cheese on mostly government bread.

In just a few short years the shame quotient has dropped considerably; now it's hard to find a person over the age of 30 in the dating pool who has not thrown away $35 in at least one stab at Match.com. The only people who still think online dating is somehow shameful or weird are the smugly-married and the sadly-never-to-be. Everybody else just thinks it's a hopeless waste of time.

But for a writer, valuable nonetheless.

Each time I've tossed up my hands and gone back to online dating I've learned something—about men, about life, about how to upload photographs that will not make you chubby. At this point I could give a course on the subject, which might be one way of making all that money, dished out in thirty-dollar increments, pay off.

Done properly Match.com is like an entire decade's worth of dating experience shoved into a few, short months. If you married early, if you settled down at a tender age and now find yourself out in the dating world, Match is definitely for you. You can race through the seven stages of romance—giddiness, companionship, creeping boredom, disillusionment, anger, breakup, chocolate cake—in the space of a week, all without having to leave your house or shave your legs.

**

Diary of my first month on Match:

Lesson One: Let Them Come To You.

I post a short profile, toss up a picture and forget about it, having decided not to care too much or knock myself out. Within minutes of posting, though I receive what Match calls a "Wink" from some guy whose member name is something like Totally Awesome Dude.

Lessons Two and Three: Judge A Book By Its Title and Pay No Attention to Winks.

I cannot take Totally Awesome Dude seriously and so delete him. Moreover, if a man cannot bestir himself to type even so much as "How r u?" it is not a good sign. Some sociologist should really study this wink phenomena; I receive hundreds of these things over my time on Match, some from men as far away as Texas, California and even England. Do women really respond to these things? What do they say—"Hi there! Something in your eye?" Are these men even serious, or just playing some kind of game? Are they like kids in a candy store, unable to keep themselves from fingering all the Snickers and Baby Ruths though they know damn well they haven't got the cash to buy?

Toward the end of Day One I receive a very nice email from a white man who says he knows he's too old for me but just wanted to send along his compliments. I check his profile; he looks a lot like Euell Gibbons and is old enough to know who Euell Gibbons was before Grape-Nuts. I send along a thanks-but-no-thanks email, operating under the belief that anyone who bothers to send an email deserves the courtesy of a response. This belief will wither upon further experience. But for now I'm Emily Post.

A few more winks over the next few days but no emails, and so finally, out of boredom, I actually open one of the winks and check the profile.

Lesson Four: Hide Your Own Profile Before Looking At Others.

This is because Match, for some dastardly reason, shows you who's peeked at your profile. Why would you want to see who has looked, and then rejected, you? Why would you want to leave a similar trail?

At any rate, this guy who winked looks vaguely interesting (although white) so I hide my profile then check his out. It begins, "I'm a vegetarian, I don't watch TV and I don't smoke."

People who "don't watch TV" make my fingernails hurt. People who go around bragging about not watching TV (or not letting their children watch or not owning one) make me want to walk up to them, stand in their face and break out into the *American Idol* theme song, which I don't even know but which I want to learn for that purpose if nothing else. And if this guy's holier- than-thou declaration was not enough I see that he is 45 and has never been married.

Lesson Five: Consider Only The Widowed or Divorced.

Naturally this lesson applies only to women of a certain age, looking for men of a certain age. I have yet to meet a man—black, white or brown—over the age of forty who has never been married who is not broken in some serious and probably unfixable way. I don't mean damaged; we're all damaged: scratched up here, dented there, lumpy where the patch was made. No, I mean broken—or possibly just mal-manufactured on the assembly line. Egg or chicken, chicken or egg, it all amounts to the same.

But if, gentle reader, you decide to disregard this ad-vice and date a never-married man, proceed with caution. The man in question will be charming, intelligent, funny as hell. You will swoon to talk to him. Don't bother asking why he has never married; he'll bring it up himself, and be defensive. Don't get into it with him, just smile and nod and go along for the ride. It'll be over soon enough.

A corollary to this lesson is to be careful too of the multi-married. I had a brief email back-and-forth with a tall (good), white (eh), writer (good) who had been married twice and who listed his current status as separated. When I expressed hesitation around this unsettled point he responded with a long, convoluted email in which he described his most recent marriage as "toxic," himself as too trusting, too talented and far too kind, laid out his plans for "self-healing" (daily yoga and meditation and trips to a Chinese herbalist who promised he would learn to forgive) and informed me he didn't want to know about my own "marriages" but did want to hear about my kids, since that was "who you are." As a helpful example, he included five paragraphs about his own progeny.

A rule of thumb regarding the multi-married: divide the number of years over thirty years old by the number of marriages and take the results. Fifteen is okay; under twelve, be careful. Anything under ten: run, run, run.

After the initial flurry of activity, things settle down. One morning I get an email from John. What John looks like I do not know because there is no photo.

Lesson Six: No photo, no chance.

There are only two reasons a man does not post his photo on a dating site: one, he thinks himself too unattractive to compete and two, he's married. But let's be real —how many men really think themselves unattractive? Answer: none.

I read John's email; it sounds like something written by a marketing firm. "Hi, I'm a SWM, 52, 6'2", 200 lbs, brown hair and eyes, considered attractive. I work professionally for a financial firm and enjoy lots of different interests, cultural and otherwise, including concerts, theater, museums, movies and travel. A sense of humor and a love of dessert are attributes I find attractive!"

From this I calculate the chances of him being married at roughly sixty percent, and the chances of him being a tool at close to one hundred. Delete.

The following day another no-photo, this one bearing the subject line "Lightning Strikes!"My finger hovers over the delete button when I chance to read the top of his profile and see that he is black. Well, I guess I can spare the time to read his email. He correctly identifies not only the novel from which I've taken the passage in my profile, but the complex emotions and themes being explored therein. Well, I guess I can read his profile. No harm in doing that much.

He is 6'7 inches tall and divorced. He is a world traveler who earns in the "above $100,000" range and has children living at home. He speaks Italian and a little French. My heart does a little doughy around my chest.

Lesson Seven: If Something Sounds Too Good To Be True....

I send a flirty little email exploring a bit further the novel in question. Then, almost as an afterthought, I ask why he has no photo on the site.

He responds, "I just thought a photo was not necessary for conversation between like-minded souls."

Well, no, I guess it's not. It's just nice.

"Even had you not provided a photo I could tell from your words that you were a sensual, sensuous, passionate, intense woman who loves deeply and wants to be loved in the same way."

Wow. Really? I say that's cool and beautiful and also something of a relief.

"I was worried because a lot of men who don't post a photo are really married. They don't want their wives finding out. Or their wives single friends stumbling over the picture. I'm so glad that's not the case here."

Hello? Hello?

Over the next few weeks come a wave of winks. One from an older white man with dreadlocks. Urn, no thank you. One from a brother whose profile begins, "I consider myself a very confident person. Some people say I'm self absorbed." Really? Astonishing.

Lesson Eight: Don't Talk About The Ex

I receive a few nice emails. One from a white lawyer who seems kind but looks like Jerry Falwell. Another is from a brother who puts his height at five-foot eight. Since I'm five-ten—and since most men lie about their height, which puts this guy at five-seven, max -1 politely decline. (Yes, shallow.) A third from a man who gives a third, and valid, reason for not posting a photo: he teaches high school. He does send one along with his email and I open it: he looks like the gym teacher I had in junior high. To all these I respond with a short thanks-but-I- don't-think-we're-compatible email, which feels awkward but more kind than silence.

A lot of men have the word "drama" planted in their profiles, as in, "NO DRAMA" or "I don't want drama" or "I'm so sick of drama I could puke." I wonder about the effectiveness of this advertising strategy. Do drama queens think of themselves as such? Do women think, "Well, he was cute but he doesn't like drama so I guess I'll move along." What exactly does drama entail, anyway? Plotting, screaming, manipulating? Asking for the remote?

As the third week ends and the emails slow down it occurs to me that perhaps my reasoning has been flawed. After all, if I'm a quality person and I'm simply sitting and waiting for others to come to me, aren't other quality people doing the same? Maybe the only ones out there trolling are the less-than-desirables. If you want something in life shouldn't you go out and get it? Isn't that what strong black women do?

Lesson Nine: Go After Them

I decide to upgrade my energy investment a bit. I will spend, max, fifteen minutes conducting a search and if I find anything interesting will send a brief email and forget about it, not caring whether the person in question responds or not. Stunningly this works. The man in question responds, wittily. For three days we write back and forth, talking about movies and musicals and basketball.

Lesson Ten: Get Out of The Virtual World

But when I suggest we meet for coffee he gets wacky. Instead of responding to my invitation, he sends along cryptic emails detailing cute sayings by his three-year- old. "The sky is full of marshmallows!" "Watch out for the undertoad!" Etc. This is charming at first. Then, not so much. Then, not at all. When I re-extend the invitation he simply disappears.

This will happen more than once during my online sojourns: a connection that seems promising will begin, surge and then tumble off a cliff. Eventually I will come to believe there is a significant subset of men (and maybe women, but I don't know about that) for whom a virtual relationship is the ultimate relationship, free from all the messiness and danger of the fleshly world. That some of these men are married seems likely, but I don't think all of them are, or even most. Some people are just socially awkward and prefer to interact solely through a computer screen. Some people are just whack.

Lesson One, Reinforced: Let Them Come To You. You don't have the time to waste.

**

So, yeah. Online dating kinda sucks.

On the other hand, if it weren't for online dating most single women over the age of forty (or maybe even thirty- five) would hardly date at all. The women I know who scorn it, the ones who think it's demeaning or scary or ridiculous or mostly a massive waste of time and energy (check, check, check and check, by the way) are the same women who haven't felt a man's arms around them since the last time they went home to Dad. The daddy thing isn't working for all of us. Of all the men I've dated since my divorce only three of them came to me from the non-digital world. That's roughly 1.2 dates every two years. At that rate I'd be getting birthday wishes from Al Roker before I found the love of my life.

Instead I met:

The Best Gay Friend

Eventually somebody told me about OKStupid, OK- Cupid, a

supposedly hip, happening and most importantly, free, online dating site. Why hand over your credit card to have your picture perused and rejected by hundreds of loser guys when you can get the experience for nothing? Why pay to be demeaned and humiliated when you can have it all for free!?

OKCupid—for all of you smug married people and people in loving relationships and people who have given up and spent some obscene amount of money on a tiny, neurotic dog you named after a Russian literary character and take to bed at night—has advanced the art and science of online dating by not just allowing you to waste precious, God-given moments of your life sifting through picture after picture of pudgy men in baseball caps who can go easily from tux to jeans and who like riding butterflies on the beach at dawn and also the Red Sox and whose friends all consider them trusty, brave and true but also allowing you to squander the fleeting, darting seconds of your time on this earth by playing games and answering stupid questions and taking tests.

Seriously.

So on I went. Threw up the picture and a poem, no longer bothered to fill out the actual profile with all its inanities. Besides, I have determined that men rarely read profiles. What they do is look at photos and move from there.

After the usual run of emails and dead ends and computer-generated Quiver Matches with men who resembled Chucky The Doll and liked Renaissance Fairs and, in desperation and boredom, after two awkward drinks, I decide to end the misery. Which is when, of course, I see him. A good-looking black man in a black turtleneck, with a literate and intelligent profile that references making tea. Plus, he's tall.

Why the hell not.

I make the first move and message him. Later on he will reference this action so many times I will swear never to do so again. But this time I did and he responded and we set up a meeting at a very chic-chic bakery/coffee spot in the South End. One of those places where a cupcake costs as much as a year of college tuition. We met on a Sunday in January. Super Bowl Sunday, in fact. Which means everyone in the place was either working, female or gay.

I am not one of those women who prides herself on her gaydar. For the first sixteen or seventeen years of my life gay people did not even exist. They sprang into life when I was at Exeter, one night when a bunch of us were hanging out at the beach and I was so giddy about having survived another year at that place that my friend Jane and I ran down the beach laughing and holding hands. When we returned to the group a boy named Phillip looked up and grinned and asked, "Are you two lesbians?"

I didn't know what a lesbian was, though I put it together quickly. "Nope!" I said, fairly certain. It turned out that Jane was, though I'm not sure she knew it at the time. She teaches college now and has a lovely family.

During college in Durham I worked in a restaurant in which half the wait staff was gay, and became good friends with a man named Tom. Tom was a true Southern gentleman, a formerly-married, formerly evangelical, formerly upstanding member of his small North Carolina community until he stopped battling his real self. He lost his home and his family and his friends in the bargain but he seemed pretty happy when I knew him, and after knowing the lovely Tom I never believed that homosexuality was a choice.

Still, had Tom not told me he was gay I wouldn't have known. Suspected, maybe, but not been sure. And after moving to Boston what little gaydar I had went all out of whack. In Boston the line between gay and, um, Eastern Intellectual is pinky thin. If every effete, soft-voiced, certain-posture-holding, leg-crossing man strolling down Commonwealth Ave was really one hundred percent batting for the other team I'd have a lot more competition out here in the hunches. A lot.

Still, when I walked into the bakery and saw The BGF sitting at a table having a cup of tea, a voice in my head as confident and clear as

Walter Cronkite announced, without hesitation: "He's gay."

Not *"Hmm, if I didn't know better I might think he's gay"* or *"I wonder if he's gay"* but just straight out, flat clear, no-holds-barred: he's gay. Never before or since have I had such an instant declaration about a potential lover.

"Not the first time I've ever heard that," he said when I finally asked him. This was a few weeks later. Despite the huge, snapping rainbow flag flapping in my face I'd sat down at the cafe and we'd chatted and he turned out to be gentle and funny and kind. So when he emailed to ask me out for real I shrugged my shoulders and said yes. And on the second date (where I offered, pro forma, to pay for my dinner and he accepted) when he asked if I was attracted to him I told the truth: "I don't know." And on the third date I did the same. And on the fourth date I told him why. It was a tense moment. I held my breath. I mean, how many heterosexual men—let alone black men—would take it well if the woman in whom they were interested suggested they were gay?

Well, he did. He shrugged.

"Ever since I was a kid people have been whispering that stuff," he said. "The problem is that there are so few acceptable ways of being for a black man, so few open avenues of legitimate black masculinity. If you cuss and snarl and act up in class and treat women like dirt, you're a real black man? He spoke to me gently, but from a great moral height. I felt like a slug.

"But if you read books or speak proper English or don't cause trouble you must be gay. Isn't that correct?"

I felt like less than a slug, whatever that is. An amoeba? A leech?

"It doesn't upset you?" I ventured to ask.

He shrugged again. "It's not like you called me a pedophile."

Wow. I mean, wow. What emotional maturity! What enlightenment! And, yeah, what was I, some kind of small-minded, backwards thinking enforcer of dangerous and damaging definitions of acceptable black masculinity? Hell no, not me! I'd prove it! I'd keep going out with him!

"Oh," said my friends when I introduced them. "Oh. Well. He certainly is tall."

It lasted four months. It lasted even after he confessed that he was unemployed and had been for some time, and after I began to suspect that being unemployed did not really bother him that much. It lasted after he showed me where he lived, in a room in the apartment of a friend. A female friend. He had a lot of girlfriends, as in *girlfriends,* and he relayed that he discussed the progress of our relationship with them all the time. It lasted even after he told me his wife had left him for a woman. It lasted even after he took me out to dinner at Popeye's. And I had to drive.

It lasted right up until the night I opened the door to find him standing on my porch wearing a lavender newsboy hat with very pretty flowers on it. A hat that would have looked really cute on my daughter. When she was ten.

I know how this sounds: shallow. I know I should be a big enough person to understand that sexuality exists on a continuum and that people fall all up and down that scale. I know, and yet....

My friend Jackie said, "It wasn't the hat. If Denzel had showed up at your door wearing that hat you'd have broken your neck inviting him in."

**

Steve The Asshole Lawyer, He Who Shall Be Named

"You're not going to write about me, are you?"

It is early summer and we are strolling the warm, buzzing streets of Harvard Square. It's our third date and he is stoned, though I don't realize it. It's been twenty years since I've been around anyone who still smokes pot and I forget the symptoms: the loose-limbed amble. The faraway gaze. The rambling, goofy talk. I think he's just being weird.

"I don't know." I smile to show I'm flirting, because he's also tall and good-looking and educated and accomplished and driving a vintage Mustang that makes everybody stop and look. My car is a minivan.

"Are you going to do anything worth writing about?" I think he'll pull me in his arms and kiss me, reassure me with his lips. Instead he says, "I'm a lawyer. I'll sue you." Then laughs to show that it's a joke.

We'd met on Match. He emailed me saying he'd just spent an hour searching through profiles and mine was the first one he'd seen and the only one which stayed with him. Something about my eyes. He was an attorney, lived just outside of Boston. He offered to drive into the city to meet me anywhere I liked. I picked a restaurant close enough to my house not to stress traffic but far enough away to feel safe in case he turned out to be some psycho who wanted to tail me home. I got there early and sat nervously in my car.

We sat at a table outside, though it was cloudy and cool for May. The waitress offered a chenille throw and I accepted, wrapped it around my shoulders like a security blanket and ordered a glass of wine.

"I hope you don't mind the suit," he said. "I came from a meeting."

Most of the men I'd met had been dressed as though to clean the gutters. If not sleep in them. I smiled. "Suits don't bother me."

He was smart, educated and confident. He could carry on a conversation without grooving the floor with his stare or jiggling his knee. On the right page politically. Square-jawed and handsome in an anchorman kind of way, which is not a way I attract most of the time.

Twice- divorced and recently out of a third serious relationship which had produced his only child. With a younger, less- educated woman.

I should have paid more attention to some of this.

By the end of the meal, after two glasses of wine, my guard had inched down. He commented on it, walking me to my car. "I'm glad you're feeling a little more comfortable. You were nervous. And skeptical."

I thought this amazingly perceptive—a man who paid attention to my feelings! I looked up (up!) at him through the drizzle, a soft, romantic mist that seemed to cut us off from the rest of the world. He was angling.

"Do you want to kiss me?" I asked.

He laughed. "Yep." And then he did, gently and sweetly and we kept it up for a few minutes, right there on the sidewalk with the rain falling gently on my face and the cars whizzing by and the sounds of the city like the background roar of a surf.

Finally I pulled away. He smiled and said, "I sure hope you're not crazy!"

Which, for some reason, sounded like a reasonable thing to say at the time, after a great first kiss and all. So, um, clearly I am.

By the next morning, though, the wine and the rain had worn off and a nagging, indefinable doubt had planted itself in the back of my mind.

On our second date he again noticed my hesitancy.

"You're back where you started in terms of not being sure about me," he said within minutes of us sitting down.

Again, I was impressed by his perceptiveness. I felt— and I remember thinking this quite clearly—that he was actually *seeing* me. When a person has spent her life feeling invisible, to be seen can be quite powerful.

After dinner he again walked me to my car and kissed me. Then he said, "Let's go to your place and talk."

I laughed. "Yeah, right."

He scrunched up his face. "Come on. I'm afraid if I let you go now I'll never see you again. I can feel your skepticism but I don't know why. I don't know what I've done, but I know that I'm a good guy and that I like you. I just want to sit somewhere comfortable and talk."

"Um, no."

"We don't have to do anything. I promise nothing will happen that you don't want to happen."

"I don't think so."

"Come on," he said. "I'm fifty-one years old."

Men in their fifties, I've noticed, are constantly stating their age. *How was your day? Okay, considering I'm 51 years old. Would you like*

223

some coffee? Sure, but I'm 56 years old. It's as if they can't quite believe what has happened to them. They thought they'd be young forever, that aging only happened to women you then got to ditch. It's shock speaking, shock and disbelief and the subconscious wish to make it go away.

We went back to my place and talked and made out a little, but I kicked him out before things went too far. In the days afterward he was in high pursuit: calling, emailing, flattering. Gradually he wore me down.

The Asshole seemed like a grown-up, a refreshing change from the overgrown boys I'd been struggling with. He had children and was participating in the raising of them, actively. He made no distinction between his biological child and his second daughter, which was tremendous. He had a real career and had also recently gotten into real estate. He did this, he explained, because he wanted to build something for his daughters' futures.

He also had a really, really nice house. A huge, well- kept, beautifully-decorated house. A house with its own plaque on the front, for heaven's sake. How could I not be impressed?

The second time we had sex he told me he loved me. I scoffed.

"That's why I didn't tell you last time," he said. "I knew you would do that."

"Because it's ridiculous."

We hadn't known each other two months, barely knew the names of each other's children or what the other one liked for breakfast. Love? At most it was infatuation. Or just plain lust.

"Come on, don't do that. I'm fifty-one! I know what I feel."

By July he was deep into this position: that he loved me, that I just needed to learn to open my heart. It was true something held me back, but I knew it wasn't caution (hello? Austin?). What it was, though, I couldn't quite put my finger upon. I thought maybe it was his still-messy situation with the Ex. Or maybe it was race, that whole the-average-unenlightened-white-man-could-never- completely-understand thing. Having been beaten into a corner by the Love Is Colorblind! Mob I was trying to give it a try, but maybe my gut wasn't going along.

I met his friends, one of whom actually knew my work and couldn't believe her buddy was dating A Famous Writer. I couldn't believe she thought I was A Famous Writer. They were a strange little circle, outside my experience: a group of weirdly-close, well-to-do professionals (doctors, veterinarians, etc), all childless except Steve, all consistent pot-smokers. They clearly loved The Lawyer and embraced me and I slowly let myself be embraced.

Meanwhile The Asshole Lawyer kept up his persuasion. He wined and dined me (and always, always, picked up the tab). He played that Regina Spektor song about never loving with both feet off the ground as we lay in his king-sized bed in his designer bedroom and kissed beneath the breeze of the ceiling fan (there's one artist ruined for me forever). He got his friends (the wives) involved in the persuading: *He talks about you all the time! He's never dated anyone like you before! He's crazy about you! Take a chance!*

I just kept saying, "Nope, not believing it," but of course deep down inside I was thrilled. He loved me! I was loveable! I was loved!

By September I was starting to bend. We took a long weekend in Montreal and he arranged everything: the hotel (which was chic and fabulous), dinner at several amazing restaurants, days spent wandering that lovely, cosmopolitan city and visiting museums and churches. At night we made love and on the drive home after the weekend I turned to him and said, "I think I might be in love."

He grinned. "Think?!"

A week or so later he went on a business trip to Las Vegas and texted me ten times a day. "I miss you so much my bones ache."

I thought: this is it. Funny how life works out, isn't it?

But...there were bumps. He smoked a lot of pot. I smoked it alongside him once or twice but quickly remembered why I'd never really taken to it even in college: it made me queasy and paranoid. But all his friends toked up routinely and he insisted that at least half of my friends were doing the same. I said I thought I knew my friends better than he. He all but patted me on my head and called me naive.

Then there was the whole race thing. He had never dated a black woman before, had no black friends or even co-workers, read no black authors or consumed black media, had never considered the overwhelming whiteness of his life. In fact, he had never considered the whiteness of himself.

"I don't think of myself as white," he told me.

"I know. That's kinda the definition of white privilege."

"I don't think of myself as privileged."

"I know."

Sometimes these discussions got a little heated. Sometimes, I'll admit, I was the one who heated them. Most times, probably. He would say something cringe- inducing about public schools (his kid went to Catholic institutions) or certain neighborhoods or the political structure of his little suburb and I would disagree and he would suggest I only thought *X* because I was ***black,*** whereas he thought *Y* because he was ***right*** and then I'd pry open his mouth and leap down his throat. He was not mean or terrible or a racist; far from it. He was just willfully oblivious.

Baldwin wrote: "No one is more dangerous than he who imagines himself pure of heart: for his purity is, by definition, unassailable."

Once he invited me along with him and his friends on their annual (slumming) excursion to a nearby stock car race. This sounded just about as much my kind of scene as a meeting of the White Citizens Council, but I wanted to be a good sport.

"Sure," I said. "Guess I'll be the only black person there!"

He dismissed this idea. "No, you won't."

So off we went to the race track in his massive pickup truck, the gang toking and giggling like teenagers. We got there and spied the cut-offs and smelled the beer and listened to the friendly-enough crowds roaring for a crash and the Asshole Lawyer looked around in astonishment and said, "You're the only black person here!" He had been attending for years and never noticed it.

By Thanksgiving the cracks were widening, though I didn't know why and I couldn't seem to shovel fast enough to keep them filled. We fought over something stupid at Thanksgiving, then made up. The rest of the holiday was tense and awkward. On Christmas Day he gave me the best present anyone has ever given me: an autographed, first edition copy of Baldwin's *Nobody Knows My Name.* I screamed when I unwrapped it.

I am not a screamer. We made love afterward but still things were strained.

All the time I felt increasingly desperate. I asked my friend The Rabbi: if I keep saying it's love but it doesn't feel like love, what does that mean? Does that mean I don't know what love feels like? Does that mean there's something deeply wrong with me?

One night we went out to dinner with one of his couple pals and the husband and wife were all gushy and handsy with each other while The Lawyer and I sat stiffly side by side. And at one point we were all laughing and discussing something and the Lawyer, trying to convey his perception of my opinion, screwed up his face and raised his voice.

"Kim was just like nayananan nanan nanay,"he mimicked. Everybody laughed. I smiled too though I was chilled. I just sat there the rest of the night and then went to his house and climbed in his bed and woke up the next morning and drove home, feeling lost inside.

Looking back now at that moment, that moment which has seared itself in my mind, I see clearly what I would not allow myself to see at the time: the Asshole Lawyer not only didn't love me. He didn't even *like* me. Not at all.

Still, we slogged along for another few weeks, until one day I received an email from him. By the time I got through the first sentence, which I don't remember, my heart was pounding so painfully I had to stop. I forwarded it to my friend Susan, then deleted it from my PC.

"Read this and tell me if it means what I think it means," I begged her.

She read it. "It's not that terrible."

"Don't tell me what it says, just if he's dumping me."

Susan said, "He needs some time."

"He's dumping me. By email."

"You should read it."

But I couldn't. I could not do if, it felt as if something terrible would happen if I let those words into my body, something would rip wide open and I'd not be able to close it and I would bleed to death. This sounds dramatic, I know, but the heart can't distinguish drama from the sound of a lion racing toward you through the undergrowth. I am a woman who has traveled alone in third- world countries and interviewed drunken warlords and covered riots in the streets, but I was too terrified to read that email. I never read it all the way.

A therapist once told me, "When you're a child and you lose love it's a life or death situation. A child who is not loved is not protected and an unprotected child can literally die. So a child who has felt that terror grows up to be an adult who still feels, really feels, as if she might die when love is stripped from her."

I picked up the phone and dialed The Asshole Lawyer but he did not answer. I left a message and waited a little while and when he didn't return my pleading voice mail I called again. And again and again and again until he turned his phone off. By this time I was, to put it clinically, freaking out. Anger, disagreement, disappointment, loss—these things I can handle, for better or for worse. But not abandonment. Abandonment just pushes me over the crazy edge.

It was evening by this time. The kids were in the dining room, doing their homework at the table and laughing about their days and I was in the kitchen, supposedly making dinner but really speed-dialing The Asshole over and over again. For a good ten minutes I paced the floor, trying to figure out who I could get to come over and watch the kids for a couple of hours while I jumped in my car and sped down 1-93 and tracked The Asshole Lawyer down at one of his haunts and screeched at him like an angry, wounded banshee with another banshee on her back. It was just the grace of God that I couldn't think of anyone.

It's funny how people can hurt you, even when you think you've protected yourself. That's because really what you've done is merely put the safety on the weapon before handing it to them. There's nothing really to keep them from taking the safety off.

It took awhile to get over the hurt of The Asshole Lawyer, but today I bear him no ill will. Really, I don't.

A couple of things helped with that. One was realizing that even he did the best he could given who he was, and he showed me who he was almost instantly. It was my bad for not paying attention. The second thing was an email I finally sent him after all repeated attempts to talk to him on the phone, just talk to him, were coldly rebuffed. One morning I had a brainstorm: I opened an email to him with the subject line: Health Issue. I left the body of the email blank. Then I hit send.

He called within the hour. I did not respond.

Then, maybe a year later, while procrastinating on the computer one morning I typed his name into a search engine, just to see what came up. What came up was a tiny item in the local paper. In the police blotter.

It turned out a man by the name of The Asshole Lawyer had been charged with disorderly conduct and vandalism after a strange altercation in a local superstore parking lot. According to the newspaper item, the man told police his truck had "backed up unexpectedly" and struck a woman's car. The woman and a friend were returning to their vehicle when the incident took place, and complained to the man behind the wheel. In response he—and here I should quote directly—profanely accused them of being sexually promiscuous and told them to "go back to the ghetto,' according to the women. A witness confirmed their story that So-and-So then grabbed a shopping cart and rammed it against their car door."

Well, alright then. Recovery from heartbreak complete.

**

The Black Nationalist was a graduate student at Harvard who sent me an email about my work on a local black-oriented television program and wishing me well. I thanked him. We became occasional email friends.

After who-knows-how-long of this he mentioned that he would be in the area of my office one day and invited me to meet. I went to Starbucks expecting a twenty-year-old child looking for some mentoring guidance. What I got was a forty-something-year-old combination of Urkel and Stokely Carmichael.

I say forty-something because he claimed not to remember his actual age. He had stopped counting in his twenties, when, during a stint in the Navy, he found himself in West Africa, had a life-altering revelation about his inherent Africanness, changed his name from something like Leroy Jackson to something like Shaka Zulu Toure X and became an honorary member of some West African ethnic group which, according to him, did not keep Roman calendar time. He grew locs and filled his closet with dashikis and grand boubous and labeled himself a Born-Again African. He said it twice when he told me, to make sure I got the joke.

The Black Nationalist, it turned out, had been pursuing his PhD for some time, perhaps because he seemed to only work on his thesis about ten minutes a day. The bulk of his time he spent blogging on the internet. Somebody had to man the front, apparently. Of course, frontmanning was not a well-paying position. As far as I could determine he lived in his office and was, officially, broke.

Our first date was coffee; he got there early and stayed seated at the table when I went to the counter to buy myself a cup. For our second date we met at a restaurant where he ordered club soda, only. On our third date he offered to meet me at my house. When he arrived, on foot, he asked if I had any food in the house. Ever the good girl (he was a starving grad student after all, slaving away in the cause of Black Liberation. The least I could do was to feed him.), I made us a dinner of mushroom omelets and green salad with dried cranberries and a little shaved parm, and afterwards as I was cleaning up he went into my living room, stretched out on my couch and went to sleep. When I suggested this was not the kind of romancing I had in mind he seemed bewildered. "But it's because I feel so comfortable here. Isn't that a good thing?"

The Spy didn't love me, but I could easily have loved him.

We met at the New Year's Eve party of a friend in Washington, D.C. I saw him watching me from a corner of the room as some other guy was chatting me up. He was good-looking and mysterious.

When he made his move toward me I kicked off my heels because I was taller. We stood talking for a while, then drifted apart, then met again in the kitchen, then drifted apart again. As the party wound down we ended up talking on the couch. I told him there was something familiar about him. He suggested I was confusing him with his brother, who I knew from a newspaper where I'd once worked. I said, no. That wasn't it.

My friend throwing the party told me later that the vibes coming off the two of us were nearly visible. She shooed the few remaining stragglers into the kitchen and closed the door to the living room where we talked, leaving us alone. I didn't notice.

Finally he said, "I know where we know each other from. Did you go to Phillips Exeter?"

It turned out we had actually been in the same class, though we didn't know one another. Or rather, I knew him but he had not known me. He'd been gorgeous then and was gorgeous now and had left Exeter after his junior year and gone on to a hundred other interesting things, the latest of which was working for the State Department in Algeria. Doing financial stuff".

"In other words, you're a spy," I said.

He laughed. "If I were, would I admit it?"

He lived a few doors down and we walked to his house and took his dog for a walk and then he walked me back to my friend's, where I was spending the night. He asked if he could see me before I left the next day and I agreed.

In the morning he woke me with a text, then came to take me to breakfast. We spent the whole day together, talking and walking around Washington and, when the time came for me to head to the airport for my late afternoon flight he said, "Stay."

It was a wild, impetuous request and any other time I couldn't have even considered it. But the kids were spending the week with their father and his lady love and his family in perfect, Ozzie-and-Harriet communion, as far as I knew anyway, and the only thing waiting for me back in Boston was a lot of dingy snow and an empty house.

"Okay."

That evening we went to his friend's house for a New Year's Day meal of black eye peas and cornbread and collard greens for luck. Be careful what you do on New Year's Day, my mother used to tell us.

Because whatever it is, you'll be doing it all year. For maybe the first time in my life I prayed the old superstition was true.

We slept in the same bed but did not have sex. The next day he drove me to the airport and promised to come visit in Boston the following weekend. He had a month before he had to return to Algeria and he wanted to spend some of that precious time with me. I arranged for the kids to spend the weekend with their father and went out and bought some perfume.

It was all so hopelessly romantic. Emphasis on hopeless.

We talked all week by phone and it was great. But from the moment I picked him up at the airport in Boston the following weekend something was off. On the way home from the airport we stopped at a restaurant for a drink. At the bar, we ran into a man I knew from the television show I do here on the local PBS station.

"Wait, you're on television?" the Spy asked.

"Just a little. Hardly at all."

We got to my house, my modest colonial. He stared at it as if it were the Taj Mahal.

"This is your house?"

"Well, half of it."

On the way upstairs we passed my bookshelves and he pointed to my books.

"How many books have you written?"

"Only three. Well, four, but the fourth was just a co-writing gig."

Maybe you can see where this will lead.

What I didn't know at the time, but later pieced together, was that the Spy had recently suffered a financial reversal of fortune, and that in some way or another a woman was involved. What I did not realize was that I was trying to drink from a poisoned well.

At one point during the weekend it snowed. We went out together to shovel the walk and he asked how I managed the long sidewalk that ran in front of my house during heavier snows.

"Sometimes I just do it myself, me and the kids," I said. "But my neighbor, who is an incredibly good guy, also helps. He has a snow-blower and if things are really bad he'll clear the walk and the drive."

"I see," said the Spy. "You just bat your eyes at him and it all works out."

The good news is by this time I had stopped giggling like an idiot when men said veiled and hostile things. The bad news is that I still wasn't picking up God's hand signals.

"Urn, actually he's just a really nice guy who helps everybody."

The Spy just smiled.

Later on he got more specific. "You don't need anyone, do you?"

"What?"

"You've got your house and your career and your children and there's nothing anybody can do for you. You're all set."

I don't really remember the rest of the discussion, mostly because I was focused on restarting my heart. Probably I said something about there being a difference between needing a partner and wanting one, about emotional and psychic support being as important as financial, about love versus need. Possibly I said something about how I'd always thought it was a good thing instead of bad that a woman should bring financial independence into the relationship, didn't he? I know I said something about how amazing he was, how much I admired the way he viewed the world as open to him, how much I liked his easy confidence at negotiating it. And his perfect French and his mechanical mind and his broad shoulders and his sexy, sexy smile. I know I said all that. Or at least I know I tried.

On the way to the airport he picked a fight over something stupid and I obliged by fighting back and then he got on the plane and flew away. We tried talking a bit afterward—I called him and he didn't answer, he called me and I was too pissed—but, really, that was pretty much that.

"It's not supposed to be this hard," said another guy I dated once.

"It's supposed to be easier than this."

I understand what he meant. Certainly that's what we're all taught, that we'll meet The Right One and Fall In Love and everything will be effortless. That's what we're taught and that's what we want desperately to believe, maybe men especially. We like to think that women are the romantics but that's just another lie. Women are far more practical when it comes to love than men.

What I know is that nothing worthwhile in my life has ever come easily. Not childhood or adolescence, not being a woman or being black. Not being married or getting a divorce, not raising children or being a daughter or being a real and trustworthy friend. Certainly not writing; writing is like sitting down at the table every morning and squeezing an ounce or two of blood upon the page. Nothing worthwhile in my life has ever been easy and so I guess I don't expect a real, grown-up kind of love—a sustained and sustaining partnership between two people, one of the most worthwhile things in all of humanity—I don't expect that to be anything less than serious work.

Uncle Jimmy said, "Love does not begin and end the way we think it does. Love is a battle, love is a war. Love is a growing up."

**

The Stalker was tall and handsome and bearded and unambiguously male. The Stalker I met for a drink on the day I came back from an emotionally-involving trip to California to see the family and so I was jetlagged and weary and hadn't eaten much and I made the mistake, after the first drink, of confessing that I did not, in fact, have plans to meet friends for dinner later and so, yes, I could stay and have dinner with him. Then I made the further mistake of getting teary-eyed when the topic turned to my recently-seen mother. Getting teary on a first date either sends a man scurrying toward the door or makes him believe he has magically touched some soft, vulnerable place inside of you like no one ever has. Believing they have breached the cool, outer shell of an attractive woman to touch the gooey softness inside is like catnip to men. I will have to remember this

After dinner he walked me to my car and opened my door and then stood there talking until I literally begged to go home to sleep. By the time I reached my house he'd texted me three times about how magical the evening had been. By the time I brushed my teeth he'd texted me twice more, announcing that he had begun the work of Googling me and reading my articles. Around 2 in the morning I was awakened by a text saying he'd just read my *New York Times* piece about not dating white men and was worried about what this meant for us. I turned off my phone and went back to sleep.

The next day he texted me so many times my mailbox filled to capacity and stopped accepting messages, something which had never happened before or happened since. Now I'd take this kind of behavior as God's big hands frantically waving me off but at the time I thought it was kinda sweet and flattering. Sure, it was a bit over- the-top but you couldn't blame a guy for being enthusiastic. It was nice, after the coolness of The Poet and his ilk to have some energy. Boy, I'd really rocked his world, huh?

On our second date he took me to a lovely tapas place down on Newbury Street and kept trying to walk with his arm around my waist. I'm not big on public displays of affection, even with those to whom I feel affectionate. He told me he'd been at a Fourth of July party right after our first date at which a friend had tried to set him up with someone.

"I told him, nope, no way, I was all set. I'd just found the woman of my dreams."

He reached across the table for my arm and began to stroke it. This had happened before. Like before I let him stroke for a second or two then pulled away.

"This is only our second date," I pointed out.

"But when you know, you know," he said.

What I knew was that it was never going to work out the way he wanted. But when he drove me back to my car (we'd met at a neutral place) and turned off his engine and began kissing me I did not pull immediately away. I was lonely and sad and aching for intimacy and love and so we made out a little in his car, but then I stopped it and told him that if we had sex it would only be sex, and I would never see him again afterward. I know this is a terrible thing to offer a man. He thought it was a test.

"I'll wait," he said, nobly. "You're worth waiting for."

"This is not a test," I said.

"I don't believe you."

"Um, really, it's now or never."

"I don't believe you."

I shrugged and got out of his car. By the time I got home my cell phone was on fire with angry, bitter recriminations and they kept up throughout the night. It was a wake-up call, a slap in the face. Here I was going along smugly confident in my ability to judge whether a man was safe or not, but here a guy I had considered a bit high-strung but harmless had morphed into a raving lunatic. A raving lunatic who might have that minute been in my bed.

I turned off my phone and got down on my knees to thank a God who watches over children and fools.

The next day he sent me a series of angry emails again accusing me of being afraid and all kinds of other crazy stuff. At first I stupidly responded; I have this really bad tendency to not want to let people get away with their irrational attacks on me. But after a while common sense took over and I stopped responding. Eventually he went away. Or so I thought.

A week or so later he emailed, saying he'd made a mistake, both in not sleeping with me and in becoming so angry and that he wanted another chance. I didn't respond, but that didn't stop him. Over the next few weeks he emailed and texted me repeatedly. I deleted them all without responding, figuring eventually he'd take the hint.

But when I mentioned, laughing, this craziness to my therapist, she did not laugh.

"He sounds obsessive. Does he know where you live?"

"No."

"But he does know where you work, right?"

To that point I had been thinking of The Stalker mostly as an annoyance. Like a lot of white guys I knew he was educated but oblivious, completely unaware of his own cushy, twin privileges and the narrow, racial, economic, geographic and political non-diversity of his life. He thought Boston really was the Hub of the Universe and anything south of New York or west of the Berkshires was like Outer Mongolia. He thought everybody lived and felt and thought the way he and his friends did, except when they didn't, in which case they existed mostly to keep him and his friends amused. He hated talking about race, wished it would just go away, even though his attraction to me was, I suspected, as much about the Excitement of The Other as anything. He was pretty sure he knew what my feelings were better than I did and his refusal to accept no for an answer only proved all of the above.

But now I was worried.

"He knows where you work," stressed my therapist. "He could just show up out of the blue."

I chuckled nervously. "Oh, that wouldn't happen." She gave me a look. "Read the paper yesterday?"

In fact I had, but I didn't know to what she was referring until she told me: a man had shot and killed his pregnant girlfriend after an argument, then shot her sister as she tried to run away. It was all over the news, but I hadn't really paid attention. I hadn't taken it in.

A day or so later it happened again, this time not in Boston but in the Western part of the state, a young, pregnant woman stabbed to death by her boyfriend. And in Connecticut. And in Florida. I saw, in fact, that it was happening all the time. Constantly.

I began reading, which is what I do when I get anxious or nervous or bored or anything. I learned: on average three women (and one man) a day are murdered by their intimate partners in America. I learned: two-thirds of violent attacks against women are committed by somebody they know, either intimate partners or husbands (2128 percent, statistics vary), acquaintances (35 percent) or other relatives (5 percent). I learned; black women experience domestic violence at a rate 35 percent higher than white women. I learned that a lot of statistics about violence again women are hard to judge because so many women never even report their rapes/attacks/batterings.

Well, shit.

Never in my life had I felt afraid of a man known to me. Unknown men, sure. Any girl who passes the age of sixteen without knowing, in a real and bone-deep way, how vulnerable she is out in the world among men is either the daughter of some vicious third-world dictator or just hopelessly daffy. I matured early; men were honking at me on the street by the time I was eleven. Even then I knew enough to be more scared than flattered, and to not take it personally. I remember walking home from the corner store once when a man yelled something solicitous out his car window as he passed. At home I asked my mother why he would do such a thing: I didn't think myself pretty even when I tried but that I wasn't trying, was wearing slouchy old clothes and had my little snatch of hair wrapped up in those spongy pink curlers.

My mother waved her hand. "He ain't interested in your hair."

In college I was hyper-aware of not getting drunk at frat parties, made easier by the fact that I stopped attending them after September of freshman year. When I moved to Philadelphia, my first big city, I was so anxious I took a self-defense class and only considered apartments above the second-floor. When I finally found the place I'd eventually lived I walked around the neighborhood for a while until I spotted an older black woman, and I asked her if I lived there would I be okay. I was asking not just about my safety from men but my safety from white folks, since it was a white, ethnic neighborhood in a little Bucks County town. She understood both unasked questions and told me I'd be fine.

When I moved to New York I was, at first, so terrified of going down into the subway I tried to take only buses to wherever I needed to go. That lasted about two weeks. To this day I am constantly vigilant in parking garages and hikes in public parks and stepping out of my car in my own driveway late at night. It took nearly a year for me to learn to sleep soundly after M moved out of the house. I switched my bedroom from the master room at the back of the second floor to the closet-sized room at the top of the staircase; I didn't want anyone breaking into the house to get to my children before they got to me. I have a sophisticated alarm system, a dog and several instruments of defense beside my bed and still the slightest thump can rip me from my bed.

But I have never been afraid of a man whose name I know. Maybe this is one upside of having grown up without a steady male presence. I never felt physical intimidation from anyone with three legs, as the old folks say. My uncles never lifted a finger against us, my mother was vigilant about not having boyfriends around her girls. My baby brother was usually on the receiving end of any punches or smacks.

M was never anything approaching violent; all of the guys I dated before and after marriage had been equally mild. Most of them were so timid and restrained I could have probably taken them in a fight. They had inches and pounds, I had a temper that could flare and scorch. In a fight usually the angriest person wins.

I knew women were routinely abused and beaten and stalked but those women were...well something other than whatever I was. Weak, vulnerable, dependent, trusting, accepting. I never thought they asked for it...but maybe they accepted what was offered to them.

Except now I had Mr. Crazy Pants on my own radar screen.

The novelist Margaret Atwood asked a group of men their greatest fear concerning women. They said, "That she will laugh at me." She asked women the same question. They said, "That he will kill me."

This is not an even exchange.

The emails kept coming. I kept ignoring them, though they had begun to sound more obsessive than simply arrogant, more creepy than jerk. I did some research and stumbled upon a book called *The Gift of Fear* and rushed out to the library and brought it home and read it through in one fell swoop, thinking, "Oh my God!" I went online and ordered six copies to give to friends, and I saved one to give to my daughter when she turns sixteen.

Essentially he says: men are trained to be aggressive and persistent, women to be polite and indirect and protective of men's feelings and egos. You think you're letting him down easy; he thinks you are "just afraid" of your own powerful attraction to him, or simply playing hard to get. This combination is not good.

The next email I did not ignore. As instructed by the book I sent The Stalker an explicit and unconditional rejection: "I am not interested in any relationships with you whatsoever. Do not contact me again. I expect you to comply with my wishes."

DeBecker writes, "There is only one appropriate reaction to this: acceptance. However the man communicates it the basic concept would ideally be: I hear you, I understand and while I'm disappointed I will certainly respect your decision."

Three minutes after I sent my email The Stalker responded: "You're the sexiest, most beautiful woman I've ever kissed and I know we could be great together if you would only give it a chance."

Here's the thing about being a mother: it's no longer just your own life at stake. When you do something stupid and self-destructive the shrapnel slices right through your body and lands on your children. Sitting in that chair reading that message I had a vision of my children grieving and motherless, and all because I'd wanted not to feel alone.

Freak out.

I grabbed my purse and got in my car and drove straight over to the sleepy little police department in my sleepy little town. The pudgy, middle-aged cop who eventually ambled out to talk to me was polite but openly skeptical.

"Two dates? What'd ya do to him?"

"Listen," I said. "This is not a joke. This guy doesn't seem to be hearing me when I tell him to go away."

I was too scared to feel foolish, or rather too scared to let feeling foolish make me slink out the door.

The cop nodded. Maybe he had a daughter or a sister or somebody.

Maybe he got just a sliver of an inkling of what it was like to be a woman in this world. "Let me just run his name," he said.

Ten minutes later he returned. "Well, he's in the system. Looks like his ex-wife had a restraining order against him a few years back."

The only good news about this was that the cop had taken a step up the ladder of taking-me-seriously. Just one. But still.

"Look," he told me, "if you want to file a restraining order I can explain the process."

But I knew even without the mocking undertone of his voice that such an act would be ridiculous. I also knew that restraining orders were usually just like red capes to the bull.

"No."

"Okay," said the cop. "In that case I'd advise you to just go home and avoid all contact with this guy and not worry about it. I'm sure he'll get the message and go away. You can keep a record of any stuff he does do. Here's my card. If he doesn't calm down, if this keeps up give me a call and maybe we'll see about having someone in the (his town's) department stop by and chat."

I also knew, from DeBecker's book, that this was a bad idea. The first time a dangerous man should see the cops is when they are coming to arrest him; otherwise you just empower him. But I didn't tell this to

251

the officer. I took his card, went out to my car and prayed. Then I went home.

When I got there I checked my email and found another message from The Stalker. Heart-pounding, I opened it. It said:

"I'm sorry. That last message I sent must have crossed with yours. I understand and I'm disappointed but of course I'll respect your wish to leave you alone. I wish you the best."

It was so nearly verbatim what DeBecker wrote that I was both relieved and shaken. Somebody had been through this before.

With the exception of a friend request on Facebook a year later, I never heard from The Stalker again. God watches out for fools and children. And fools with children, apparently.

**

Right about here is where this story should wind to some conclusion. Right about here is where I should write that none of these connections worked and so finally I stopped seeking at all. Abandoned online dating. Released my desire for partnership. Focused on raising the children and enjoying my friends and doing my jobs and living my life. Learned something large and significant about myself, something that would neatly fit into a little saying for the back of the paperback. And then one day as I stood in the checkout line at the Shaw's Market this tall, good-looking black man with a tattered, dog-eared paperback of *The Fire Next Time* sticking out of his pocket bumped my cart with his. Our eyes met. He smiled.

Well, no.

The last time I was at the supermarket the person behind me was an irate old white lady who bitched about Michelle Obama telling her what to eat. "Meanwhile she goes on with her ribs and her French fries and such!"

Okay.

I have no real ending to this story, because the story has not yet come to an end. Online dating did not deliver the Man of My Dreams. Love has not yet come, and the truth is it may never, whether I look for it or not.

Some people get lucky. Some people get lucky and their luck begins at birth, by hook or by crook. They grow up knowing what love is and what it isn't, they expect it to come. Unafraid they go out into the world and choose, consciously or otherwise, good partners with whom to build that funny thing. Some people get lucky and some people never get anything at all and many more people make their peace with some lesser version of the possible. Some people, having done that once, decide they cannot do it again, decide it isn't fair to the other person or to themselves.

It's not serendipity. It's just life.

Still, one good thing about being a writer is that everything's material. And the material from online dating is wide and deep. What I found most fascinating about the process was not the pretense folks throw up, not the lies men tell about their height and their income, or the lies women tell about their age and their weight. Those are small and hopeful diversions, easily uncovered. Easily absolved.

What I found most fascinating was how much people reveal themselves online. How much we all give away without really intending to. The 48-year-old man who jokes not once but twice about being immature ("to play the sax well you need to start as an adolescent, which still gives me plenty of time, hah hah!")The writer who describes himself as modest, but sends page-long emails boasting about his writing, who some agent compared him to, how good he is at photography ("Something I do well and for which I'm paid well to do.") Out there on the runway of the internet we think we're looking fabulous but really our slips are showing and there is toilet paper stuck to our shoe.

The crudest thing I've ever done to a man I did to The Social Worker. He was the first guy I met on Match, the first man I dated after the divorce, was kind and thoughtful and attentive, a little older than I might have wanted but good-hearted nonetheless. Still, I knew pretty quickly that if I settled with him I'd be crawling right back into the same hole out of which I had just climbed.

But I was selfish. It had been more than a year since I'd felt a man's intentions, more than that if you included the painful end of the marriage. This was before The Poet, when it seemed nobody possible was showing up in real life. Also, the Social Worker was out there doing good in the world. This was important to me.

I never lied or made things up. I said I wasn't sure of my feelings, that I wasn't sure things would work out in the long run. But I also did not stop seeing him...and when I finally did I let it start again. I didn't realize then that men listen to nothing you say and only what you do. This is the opposite of women, who will ignore all manner of bold-faced, red-flag behavior because a man sprinkles out a few, sweet words.

One night, after we had broken up, I let him buy me dinner because I was lonely. The predictable happened, but when it was over and he was climbing from my bed I said, "Don't think this changes anything."

Ouch.

What's interesting is that at the time I did not think of my words as being hurtful. Or maybe it's more accurate to say I did not think of the Social Worker as capable of being hurt. I grew up in a world of wounded women who believed men really had no feelings to speak of and were largely incapable of being hurt. Certainly incapable of being hurt the way we were. For a long, long time I believed that, on some deep subconscious level, though of course I would never have admitted as much, not even to myself. It was only after my divorce and re-entry into the dating world that I came to really understand men have hearts, hearts that can be broken. Hearts that might even break over me. It was an astonishing revelation, both electrifying and terrifying and, ultimately, sobering.

Fortunately the Social Worker remains around to remind me. We are good friends now, so good he feels either entitled or obliged, every third or fourth time I see him, to remind me of my casual cruelty. Penance, I suppose.

But not believing men could be hurt is really just the flip side of not believing oneself ever being important enough to a man to cause such hurt. This is the crux of it, the buried truth.

As a young woman I'd attached myself to M, a good and decent man but wrong for me and I for him, largely because I feared no other decent man would ever love me. Twenty years later I stepped back out into the world still believing as much. The only difference was I knew that continuing to trade on such goodness was not only unfair but impossible.

Better to be alone.

So I began to date. Incrementally and haltingly at first, seeming to confirm the no-one-else-will-love-me belief. Then I went online and suddenly: deluge. Suddenly lots of men wanted me, and not the crazies and not simply for sex (not simply, I said. I am not naive.) The Social Worker, The Gay Best Friend, The Medical Professional, The Cambridge Liberal—these were good and decent men who made it clear their yearning involved the whole of me.

"You're the complete package," said The Medical Professional. "You are the prize."

This was a revelation, this idea of myself as the prize. I mean: holy crap.

Maybe it's something other women grow up knowing. Maybe it's kissed into the foreheads of fair-haired little girls by their adoring fathers, dripped into their chocolate milk by mothers who themselves feel fully worthy and deserving of love. Maybe there are two kinds of women in the world: women who grow up knowing their prizeworthiness and women who do not. Those who don't face a pretty long and arduous climb up that mountain. Some people never make it. You see their bodies broken on the rocks all the time.

It takes a lot of hard, emotional climbing to make the journey, a lot of loving confrontation with the voices outside and in. James Baldwin wrote, "'You know, it's not the world that was my oppressor, because what the world does to you, if the world does it to you long enough and effectively enough, you begin to do to yourself."

It takes nights of loneliness and mornings of survival and walks in the woods with a dog who adores you. It takes loving friends and family and some meaningful work that illuminates and sustains and endures. It takes sweet-tempered rejection of all the stupid, romantic, nonsensical clichés about love and how it arrives that people will pour on to you.

It does not necessarily take having a lot of random men express their admiration. But that doesn't hurt.

VI
HOW JAMES BALDWIN SAVED MY LIFE

The writer's greed is appalling. He wants, or seems to want, everything and practically everybody...yet in another sense, and at the same time, he needs no one at all.

James Baldwin

I was born in Memphis. I learned to read when I was five or six and then to write and pretty soon I was scribbling all over the place, mostly my name or that of our dog Mr. Carter or my first-grade teacher Mrs. Hutton, whom I routinely professed to love.

Like most women in those days my mother was given to the habit of having babies, despite her best efforts to avoid her mother's fate. In some ways she succeeded; we were all born within legal union and instead of ten there came only five, the last two of which came together, a tidy and joyful little package which included the Only Son. But what seemed a colon at the end of my parent's marriage turned into a period. My mother and father divorced when I was four and the twins still sported unclosed fontanels. The collapse of the marriage and the withdrawal of my father left us struggling and, after some time, humiliatingly poor. My mother tried to work and couldn't. She tried to keep us alive and did. The world looked on, indifferent and unmoved.

One day when I was seven or six we were at my Aunt Pearl's house, maybe visiting, maybe waiting for my mother to come pick us up after work. Aunt Pearl was my mother's aunt, which really made her my Great Aunt Pearl, but black folks in the South don't much bother with such distinctions: aunt is as aunt does. (Which is why I call James Baldwin "Uncle Jimmy" even though he was in no ways my kin.) Aunt Pearl was wiry and ageless and slightly terrifying in the way that ageless older people can be. Having never married or had children, she lived a Spartan life in a tiny, wooden shotgun house that I remember mostly as close and dim. She was also extremely generous with her time and limited resources, and she made the most delicious apricot fried pies.

It was at the back of that shotgun house, in the last room that served as a kind of mudroom/storage area, that I found the mouse. I was out there looking for something Aunt Pearl had sent me after when I spotted his tiny gray body caught in a trap. I took one look and burst into tears. By the time Aunt Pearl got there I was sobbing uncontrollably.

"Child, what in the world is wrong with you?" she demanded.

Southern black adults of my mother's and my great aunt's generations did not believe in coddling crying children. Absent bone poking through skin you probably had no good reason to be making a racket and if you did not cease they would happily give you one.

"Hush your mouth!"

I pointed at the mouse. Aunt Pearl took one glance and sucked her teeth.

"You crying about that?" She walked to the mouse, grabbed a nearby shovel and scooped it, trap and all, into a small bucket just outside the door. When she returned, dusting her hands on her faded housedress, she gave me a hairy look.

"Tenderhearted," she said, shaking her head sadly. "Better get over that."

"Yes ma'am," I said, the way I was supposed to. I had no idea what she meant about getting over it, but I certainly intended to try.

Middle children are supposed to be the forgotten ones, and it is true that I felt overlooked, though I probably wasn't, at least no more than anyone else. It felt that way because my oldest sister Louise was pretty and popular and increasingly rebellious while the next oldest, Annette, was churchgoing and obedient and good. I was none of those things, neither popular nor devout, neither rebellious nor obedient, neither left nor right and so whatever attention my overburdened mother had to give usually swung right over me. Middle children are also supposed to be peacemakers, but here the profile collapses. When we battled as children—and we battled often—I was always right there in the fray. I ranged from side to side like a mercenary, sometimes teaming up with Louise again Annette, sometimes with Annette against Louise. As the twins got older it often became two or three of us older girls against their clubby little duo. What else are closets for but to lock your brother and sister inside?

More often than not, though, I was reading. As childhood ranged along and things got tougher for us, financially, and my mother struggled to keep both us and her spirit alive and one sister drifted, or ran, toward the cliff and the other drifted, or ran, toward the church I crawled into books. As school got awkward, I crawled into books. Academically I was solid but I was also weirdly tall and wide-hipped and my hair would not grow below my ears and I had some kind of bladder problem I could not control and so once actually ended up wetting myself in the middle of class, a horrifying moment one never forgets. So I crawled into books. Our living room had a small built-in bookcase, which my mother kept lined with a prized set of encyclopedias and a dozen or so Readers Digest

Condensed Books.

The Readers Digest books I especially loved, with their rich, brightly-patterned covers and their spines with the book tides stacked one atop each other in chunky, colorful blocks and inside their tales of glamorous people and foreign lands. The idea of boiling down a novel to its most salient and sticky parts is now both terrifying and laughable to me but at the time all I cared about were the stories. During the summers I would take one to bed at night, climb under the covers and read straight through until dawn. When the night finally broke and the birds began chirping and it felt safe enough to sneak outside I'd sit on the front porch in the velvet morning and watch the sun come up and feel like I was on to something, something big. Something that might just save me.

Uncle Jimmy wrote, "You think your pain and your heartbreak are unprecedented in the history of the world, but then you read. It was books that taught me that everything that tormented me was the same thing which connected me to everyone alive or everyone who had ever been alive."

**

In our living room, in a corner on the bottom shelf of the bookcase and partially hidden by the sky-blue couch, lay a dusty stack of black and white notebooks. Nobody paid much attention to them. For most of my childhood I neither remembered nor cared about their existence. Only once, on a bored summer day around age eleven or twelve did I pull out one of the notebooks and flip through it, and found some writing in my mother's hand about something I did not understand and put it away.

When my first novel was published my Aunt Catherine told me, "You know, your mother always wanted to be a writer."

I didn't believe her. How was that something I would not know? How was that something my mother would never tell me, would never mention as I struggled to become a writer myself? Impossible.

But then I thought about all the books in our house. I considered how expensive those encyclopedias must have been, those mail-order books. I thought about what a lot of struggling divorced black mothers of five in Memphis would have done with that money. I remembered the journals down there in the dust of the bottle shelf and I knew that it was true.

Aunt Catherine said, "She told me, "Cathy, Kim is living the life I wanted to live.""

Even second-hand I knew there was as much pain in this statement as pride. Hearing it made my stomach clutch with sadness but I did not cry. Tenderhearted I once was, but I got over it.

**

Somewhere between elementary school and junior high I discovered the public library. There was a local branch not far from our house but the main library was in downtown Memphis, a low-slung building that overlooked the Mississippi and stood not far from the main Post Office. The post office was the place my mother worked, the mysterious building full of white people into which she disappeared while we sat in the car with Aunt Pearl and watched. It was the source of our food and our clothes and our modest but stable life and then suddenly it wasn't anymore. Aunt Pearl stopped coming to watch us overnight while my mother worked. My mother stopped disappearing into the post office. We stopped going downtown.

Uncle Jimmy said, "Anyone who has ever struggled with poverty knows how extremely expensive it is to be poor."

But I still had the local branch, a twenty-minute walk from our house if you walked really fast. Usually I couldn't though; I was too weighed down by books both coming and going. I always took out as many as possible, plucked them greedily from the shelves as if I were plucking ripe oranges from a tree. It felt dangerously illicit, cradling those books in my arms, strolling heavy-laden beyond the library doors. It felt as though I were getting away with something, taking something not really meant for me but which I needed to have.

The longest love affair of my life has been with books and reading, and the second longest with libraries. Since becoming an adult I've set my house and my life down in ten different cities in eight different states but I have never lived anywhere for more than a month without finding the public library. I've walked streets where I felt unwelcome or afraid, stepped into buildings in which I felt uncomfortable or alone, attended and even taught at colleges that seemed not built for me, but I have never in my life felt like an outsider in a library. When the aliens come and we are forced to make a case of the preservation of humanity, I know where to turn.

I'm not sure when it occurred to me that all those glorious books I was lugging home had not appeared on the library shelves with a wave of someone's wand, that someone had written them, some human being. Some human being not unlike myself. It must have been before eighth grade, because by then I was writing poetry, typical adolescent stuff about trees and the feel of dusk descending and the smell of leaves after the rain. Not expecting much I entered a bunch of the poems in a city-wide contest sponsored by Memphis State University, and, astonishingly, won first place. It felt like winning the Nobel Prize. My award was a golden certificate and a paperback book of poetry by e.e. cummings entitled *No Thanks*, which I still have. It sits on the shelf near my desk. I look at it when I write.

Despite the validation of that prize, I never, as a child, really considered the idea that I might actually *become* a writer when I grew up. I was The Smart One in the family and the job of The Smart One was to go off and do something Smart that could make a lot of money and help everybody out. This became especially true after I was airlifted to boarding school in New Hampshire at the age of fifteen. The only problem was, suddenly I was no longer smart. For the first time in my life the letters coming back on my schoolwork were not As or even B's. I was shocked and not a little humiliated. Also: alone, afraid, adrift.

The first year at Exeter was the worst. Every morning I woke up realizing just how far I was from anyone who cared whether I lived or died. It was bitterly cold outside, colder than I had ever experienced. And everywhere I looked were rich, white people, including the bed next to mine. My roommate was blonde, beautiful and instantly popular. She played sports I had never heard of (field hockey? lacrosse?) seemed confident in her classes and gathered friends like ticks while I could not wield a stick or ball of any kind and brought home "Ds."

Seeing all that wealth hurt me. It hurt to hear people talking about their summer homes on "The Cape" (By senior year I would respond "Which cape? Cape Horn? Cape of Good Hope? Use the damn proper name!" but at first I was too desperate to conceal my ignorance) and the summers in Europe and their fathers who loved them. It hurt to see all that and know back in Memphis my family was still heating water on the back of the stove to take a bath. It hurt and it pissed me off.

On top of everything else, someone had talked me into taking Latin as my required foreign language.

Big, big mistake.

Please allow me to dispel all those things people say about the benefits of Latin. It didn't help me on my SATs. It didn't improve my vocabulary. It didn't help me later learn French or any other useful language. All it did was suck.

The only thing I took from three years of Latin was a deep inferiority complex, a loathing of antiquity and a still-active PTSD-fear of old white men with beards. His name was Mr. Wooley and his disapproval of me—my gender, my race, my general Latin incompetence, I don't know—could not have been any more apparent had it been chiseled in Latin script across his florid face. Exeter classes are conducted around a large oval table in what is known as the Harkness method. I called it No Place To Hide.

"Try again, Miss McLarin. Perhaps your comprehension wall magically increase and astound us all."

I was drowning, but I was going down in silence, the way people do in real life. None of that thrashing and flailing they show in the movies, none of that crying and waving for help. Late at night, when the phone booth in the basement was finally empty I'd crawl downstairs and call my mother, crying and begging to come home. My mother was steely in her resolve that I would not throw away the best opportunity of my life.

Are they lynching you?

No.

Putting their hands on you in anyway ?

No.

Then stay and get whatever you can from that place. Do not let those people drive you away.

Uncle Jimmy wrote: "So that any writer, looking back over even so short a span of time as I am here forced to assess, finds that the things which hurt him and the things which helped him cannot be divorced from each other; he could be helped in a certain way only because he was hurt in a certain way; and his help is simply to be enabled to move from one conundrum to the next—one is tempted to say that he moves from one disaster to the next."

I stayed at Exeter. I stayed and dragged to class and cowered when

Mr. Wooley sneered at my efforts to translate Cicero. I stayed and cried in my room and then wiped my tears with a scowl and went out in the world, shielded by anger, cloaked in furious disdain.

"Smile!" people urged, seeing me. "Smile!"

Oddly enough, being ordered to smile rarely makes me want to do so. Oddly enough, being ordered to smile usually has the rather unintended consequence of making me want to haul off and smack the speaker in the face. Maybe this is an over-reaction to an innocent suggestion, or maybe there's something beneath the command that rightly makes my skin itch, some half-hidden belief that an unsmiling (read: unaccommodating, un-approachable, un-submissive) woman is not to be tolerated, not in the least. When I was younger and lived in New York City barely a week passed when I was not ordered to smile by some man I passed on the street, ordered, as though he had the right to do so. And, in a different tone but with the same result, urged to smile by some white woman I knew at work.

I've never heard a man tell another man to smile, only women. I've never heard a black person tell a white person to change the expression on her face. The personal is political, the past is the present, the subconscious speaks constantly. Uncle Jimmy said, "The great force of history comes from the fact that we carry it within us, are unconsciously controlled by it in many ways, and history is literally present in all that we do. It could scarcely be otherwise, since it is to history that we owe our frames of reference, our identities, and our aspirations."

Even when the order to "Smile" comes from one black person to another, or one white woman to the next, and is sincerely meant only as an urging toward happiness I wonder why in the world we think it will work? Does ordering a person in pain to stop revealing that pain make the pain cease? Does it make everything better? Or does it just make it better for you?

At Exeter no one ever asked why I was not smiling. No one paused on the beach to raise a hand to shield the sun and see if I was drowning or just fooling around. Mostly they just jogged on past, calling out for me to smile.

"I don't think I'm gonna make it," I told one of the older black girls finally. "It's just too hard."

"Girl, do not let these people get to you."

"But it hurts, being here. Seeing...all this. Doesn't it hurt you?"

She crossed her arms against her chest and snorted. "You're too sensitive. You need to let this mess run off you like water off a duck's behind."

So, I did. I made my skin impervious as best I could. I made my skin impervious and I swam for solid ground. And the first place my feet touched was English class. Even when the teachers circled my rusty grammar or underlined my wobbly typos they praised my writing, praised it high. I couldn't spell for crap but I knew what I was trying to say and how I was trying to say it, and it was good.

"Your sensitivity to human problems comes through in all your writing," wrote my first-year English teacher. "You have everything you need to be a fine writer."

I was fifteen, cast out of one ill-fitting world and into another, away from home, alone, inadequate and terrified. But I could write, damn it. I could write.

**

When I write that James Baldwin saved my life I do not mean those words literally. Nor when I call him Uncle Jimmy do I mean that he was, literally, my uncle. He wasn't, though I would have traded a raft-full of real relatives to make it so. I never even had the honor of meeting him or of hearing him speak in person, or even watching him live on television. All I know of James Baldwin I know through documentary film clips and black and white photos. And his books. His amazing books.

When I say James Baldwin saved my life I don't even mean that reading James Baldwin at certain low periods of my life rescued me from darkness or despair, though that is certainly true. I came to James Baldwin initially through his fiction, which places me in the minority of Baldwin acolytes. Baldwin is far better known for his searing, prophetic essays, but when I was younger I rarely read essays or nonfiction unless forced to. I read short stories and novels: great, serious, world-changing stuff. James and Faulkner and Steinbeck and Hemingway at first, as I was taught, and then Woolf and Eliot and O'Connor and Welty and then, finally, Ellison and Wright and Walker and Morrison and Marquez. I thought all serious people read serious novels; that working one's way through a poetic, prophetic vision of the world in this way was what it meant to be imaginatively alive. I was well into my thirties before I realized how many serious folks looked down their serious noses at fiction. I was seriously stunned.

Still, I kept on reading fiction. Life felt like nonfiction enough to endure; out on the streets of Greensboro and, later, North Philadelphia I met and interviewed and wrote about people struggling against poverty, walking in violence, suffering or raging against lousy schools, shattering and trying to hold together shattered families, carrying stunted senses of themselves. Every now and then I read some nonfiction book that would inform my reporting, such as Jonathan Kozol's *The Night Is Dark and I am Far from Home* or Alex Kotlowitz's *There Are No Children Here* but what I wanted when I came home from work and shut the door against the pain of the world was not facts or so-called reality but truth. Truth.

Which is why, at some point when I stumbled onto Baldwin's great short story, "Sonny's Blues" I thought, "Well, there it is."

By then I had left journalism and published my first novel. On book tour when people asked me for my favorite writer I said Ernest Hemingway, and not only to see the surprise twist their face. Hemingway seemed to me a perfect model: he'd been a reporter, disliked fancy writing, put things down as simply and cleanly as he could. I loved his short stories and very much liked *The Old Man and the Sea* and *The Sun Also Rises*, though some of that male agony seemed just a trifle overwrought. I also told people I loved Alice Walker and Toni Morrison, and I did, though

in a more distant and frankly intimidated kind of way.

"What about black men?" one black man asked me one day. He stood at the edge of the small crowd at the bookstore, arms crossed against his chest. "You like any black men writers?"

"Of course," I said. Drawing a sudden, terrifying blank.

He twisted his face. "No you don't. You just want to go around writing about how niggers ain't shit."

For a moment I was paralyzed. I knew, vaguely, about the lingering civil war between black male and female writers: Amiri Baraka attacking Alice Walker, etc. But those were Big, Serious Writers writing Big Serious Books and I was just starting out. Why in the world was this strange black man throwing darts across the bookstore with his eyes? What had I ever done to him?

"You can't even think of one, can you?" He sucked his teeth in disgust. "Ernest Hemingway!"

The terrible thing was, he was right. Not about writing *how niggas weren't shit*—that's just ridiculous. But he was right about the fact that at the ripe old age of thirty-four I should have been able to reel off, without hesitation or disconnect, a long list of black male writers on whose shoulders I stood. I'd read Wright and Ellison in high school and college, but neither had really resonated with me at the time, for whatever reason. I'd read Eldridge Cleaver but he just freaked me out. Malcolm made me feel guilty and Martin made me feel sad and that was really the sum of it. Somehow, terribly, I didn't know Douglass or Brown or Horton or Walker or Toomer or even, good Lord, DuBois or Hughes or Hayden or Gaines. But one name did come to mind.

"Baldwin,"! blurted out. "I love James Baldwin."

The brother heaved a breath of disgust and walked away. At the time

I didn't get it, but know I understand: misogyny and homophobia often live side-by-side.

But it was over. Somebody jumped in with another question and the talk went on and I did not fall apart. Back at my hotel I kicked off my shoes and sank into the chair. James Baldwin had saved me. I thought I should probably check him out in return.

I started with *Go Tell It On The Mountain,* his first novel. I loved the language and the music, the images and the themes but the anguished church scenes struck a little too close to home. I tried to read *Just Above My Head* but couldn't get through it for some reason. Then I picked up *Another Country.* And fell in love.

**

At Duke the praise for my writing leveled off precipitously, the teachers of English there decidedly less charmed by my work and especially my continuing inability to spell. That was okay; I was so relieved to have survived Exeter and to be back in the warm embrace of the South that nothing much could shake me, academically. I joined the student newspaper, skipped the fraternity parties and sorority rushes, moved off campus and got a part-time job working as a hostess in a local, hippie restaurant where I met my future husband and watched a lot of people snort cocaine, smoke pot and screw around. Usually not all at once.

Sophomore year I declared a double major of English and public policy, thinking I'd use the English for writing and the public policy to get a job and not be poor. I was thinking law school, not because I had the slightest interest in law but because—that's right—I wanted to not be poor. I was the third person in my family to go to college, behind my mother (who did not make it) and my sister, one year ahead of me and still pushing through. More than anything I felt obligated not to let myself or my family down, to justify the smarts I had been given. That meant becoming either a doctor or a lawyer, and I hated the sight of blood.

Duke's English department became dominated by postmodern theorists in the late 1980s but that was just after my time. Looking at my college transcript now I am stunned to realize I took not a single class in African- American or multicultural lit. Instead I took Shakespeare before 1600 and Special Topics: Satan as Hero and 20th Century British Lit. Were those classes requirements or was I a secret anglophile, secret even from myself? What's funny is that about Shakespeare before 1600 I remember zippo. Still, I guess having the canon installed was important nonetheless.

I read no James Baldwin at either Exeter or Duke.

Uncle Jimmy said, "The paradox of education is precisely this: that as one begins to become conscious one begins to examine the society in which he is being educated."

In the fall of my junior year I took a class called "Writing for the Media." On the first day of class the professor, an aging, grizzled journalist straight out of the movies, on-leave from *The Washington Post*, stood up and delivered a fiery sermon on the role of the fourth estate and the sacred responsibility of the journalist in a democratic society. Then, with a sly grin, he added, "The role of the journalist is to comfort the afflicted and afflict the comfortable."

That sat me up straight. After three years at Exeter and another three at Duke, I knew a helluva lot of comfortable people I would like to afflict.

"The journalist is the defender of the downtrodden and the watchdog of the rich and powerful," he said. "It's a sacred duty."

Seriously? I could do all that while writing? And somebody would pay me a salary? Law school, goodbye.

Someone once told me there are two kinds of people who become reporters: people who want to be Woodward and Bernstein, and people who want to be Ernest Hemingway. I went into journalism mostly wanting to be Hemingway, but not minding a little W&B in the mix. And then, for a while, because you *can* make incremental changes in the way

society operates, because the press really *is* a public trust, for a time I

thought, well, maybe I *do* want to be Woodward and Bernstein. But then,

after a little while longer, I realized: actually no. In the day to day slog of

being a working journalist the only things that gave me any pleasure at

all were the writing and the paycheck. Sometimes the traveling. Except

when the traveling involved rushing off to the scene of some

unimaginable disaster. Which, of course, it usually did.

But this is getting ahead of myself.

After that class I focused on becoming a journalist. I landed a

summer internship with the *St. Petersburg Times* in Florida, then

returned to Durham in the fall and began working for a news-aggregating

organization called Africa News. I began sending out resumes.

As a last-gasp salute to my creative writing side, I submitted a

writing sample for a special short story class taught by the noted

Southern writer Reynolds Price. When I was accepted it seemed to

confirm my growing confidence that I had something to say and some

means of saying it.

The class turned out to be populated almost exclusively by the kind

of Dukie I hated: wealthy, privileged, sophisticated and most

disturbingly, intelligent. Among them was a young man with the same last name as the university, and not by coincidence. He and all the other students affected a certain world-weariness. They had been writing for years, engaging in workshops since they were twelve and some had even already been published in small magazines. I was instantly out of my league.

Still, I vowed not to be intimidated and I was not, until the day the university heir came to class and read a story aloud. It was elegant and tightly-written, as far removed from my own stumbling as a gazelle from a slug. I was bummed.

Our semester long assignment was to write, revise and submit a short story of fifty pages or more. Mr. Price would read the stories at the end of the semester and return them with his comments.

"One more thing," he intoned in his stately Southern drawl. If we wished he would include in his notes his opinion not only of the story but of our writing talent itself. He would, in essence, tell us whether we were writers, whether we had "it" or not.

"But I will do so only if you ask," he said.

Needless to say, I was terrified. Price was not only highly-regarded among Southern literary novelists, for would-be writers at Duke he was The Man. He'd discovered Anne Tyler, for heavens sake, had plucked her from the muck of an undergrad writing class and encouraged her quirkiness and look—Pulitzer Prize! What if he thought I had "it?" What if he declared me a writer and invited me into the inner circle; wouldn't everything be wonderful? Wouldn't it be the confirmation I needed, wouldn't it seal the deal? On the other, what if he said: "No dice, kid." Wouldn't I be devastated? Wouldn't I want to just put down my pen and slink away?

Would I?

I don't know if it was cowardice or arrogance or simple self-protection but after much agonizing and gnashing of teeth I decided not to ask. I turned in my final story, a fifty-page masterpiece about an older black woman named Mattie and heaven-only-knows what, absent the request and felt a layering sense of relief at not having to face the possible end of myself when the paper came back. Only years later would it occur to me that maybe the whole exercise had been some kind of test.

Maybe Price was trying to prove that a writer is one who writes, regardless. Maybe he was making the point that if you have to ask, you aren't. Writing is hard, lonely, even dangerous work, dangerous because it requires, properly done, a way of walking through the world that allows few illusions. The great Japanese filmmaker Akira Kurosawa said something along the lines of, "To be an artist means never to avert one's eyes." This is true. The role of the writer is to stare straight into the white-hot furnace of what it means to be human in this world and for all the beauty and joy that means it also means a helluva lot of pain and confusion and suffering.

Seeing the world for what it is and other people and ourselves for what we are is not easy. There's a reason so many writers end up either drunk or walking into lakes. Try waking up in the Matrix without Laurence Fishburne there to pull your ass out of the goop and some hot chick to stare adoringly at you while you face the truth. See how you fare. Henry James advised young writers to be "one of those people on whom nothing is lost" but Henry James was rich and white and male and privileged and otherwise well-cushioned from the repercussions of his dangerous advice. Henry James can kiss my ass.

So maybe Price was making a point. Or maybe he just wanted to weed some of us out of the competition stream. Flannery O'Connor, when asked if she thought the university stifles writers, famously replied, "My opinion is that they don't stifle enough of them."

Now that I teach myself, I can see what she means.

Price eventually returned my masterpiece with a letter of criticism in which he said my story was incomplete, rife with syntactical errors and disappointing in the end. He did make note of its "good qualities: a narrative conviction and fluency, an obvious ease of invention on the author's part, an occasionally striking phrase."

"These," he wrote, "are all things that should stand you in good stead in newspaper work." In other words: don't quit your day job.

At first I was hurt, and then I was angry and then I was just hurt again. Tender-hearted, but getting over it.

**

"He was facing Seventh Avenue, at Times Square. It was past midnight and he had been sitting in the movies, in the top row of the balcony, since two o'clock in the afternoon. Twice he had been awakened by the violent accents of the Italian film, once the usher had awakened him, and twice he had been awakened by caterpillar fingers between his thighs."

Those are the opening lines from *Another Country,* lines which hooked me like a trout.

Another Country is a big, sprawling, messy novel about a group of writers and artists and musicians in 1950s Greenwich Village. It's about love and relationships, race and sex and sexuality, self-delusion and the vicious damage of that special brand of white American willful innocence that Baldwin ever decried. It's about New York.

It is not a flawless book; it's bumpy and uneven, verbose in some places and in others frustratingly rough. It is also honest and unflinching and beautiful and one of the bravest things I've ever read (another would be *Giovanni's Room.)* It is both furiously clear-eyed and wistfully hopeful about love, which is no mean feat. At that stage in my life I wondered: how in the hell did he manage that?

To find out, I stepped out of fictional haven and into the world of nonfiction. In rapid succession I purchased, devoured and metabolized every Baldwin essay I could find, beginning with those two seminal works: "My Dungeon Shook: Letter to my Nephew on the One Hundredth Anniversary of Emancipation," and "Down At The Cross: Letter from a Region of My Mind."Together these two great essays were published in 1963 under the title *The Fire Next Time.*

Fire indeed.

If James Baldwin were not gay and dead I would marry him. And really it's only the dead part that gives me pause.

**

After college I worked a series of journalism gigs, starting with a six-month stint at the Associated Press in Raleigh, moving on to three years at *The Greensboro News & Record* and then to the *Philadelphia Inquirer.* Back then the *Inquirer* was one of the holy grails of journalism, an aggressive, dynamic, big-city paper lead by the great editor Gene

Roberts and which had won something like four hundred Pulitzers in a row. Everybody wanted to work there, and when I landed a job at the tender age of 26 some of my colleagues at the *News & Record* were pretty sure they knew why.

"Nice to be black these days," one man said to me.

"About damn time," I said. Okay, not really. I only wish I had.

At the *Inquirer* I did what I was told and went where I was directed, first out to Bucks County to write about school board meetings and zoning disputes and the death of Abby Hoffman, then back into the city to cover about North Philadelphia. Out to Los Angeles during the Rodney King riots. Eventually to Liberia to cover the brutal civil war ripping that country to shreds.

I wrote a story about a North Philadelphia girl who was thriving in school despite a family that seemed determined to incorporate every possible dysfunction: mother in jail, father murdered (by the mother, as I recall), an older sister who didn't really want her, drugs and poverty and danger walking home from school. The article won me a few awards and, far more importantly, won the young woman a scholarship to a boarding school and promises of cash for college. All of which was great for her and good for me but did nothing to address the huge, systemic inequalities which produced the situation in the first place. It turned out that journalism was better at (sometimes) comforting the afflicted than afflicting the comfortable.

After a few years *The New York Times* came knocking. This was very exciting for nearly everyone except me. By this time I could no longer ignore the fact that I was, at heart, not a very good reporter, and the reason I wasn't very good was because I hated it. I hated schmoozing politicians and public relations people. I hated walking up to strangers and asking them questions. I hated sticking my tape recorder into the face of people who had just suffered loss and asking them how they felt.

The thing I liked about being a reporter, besides the occasional happy ending for a person I wrote about, was the writing. *The Inquirer* was "a writer's paper," a place where good writing was valued and a writer's voice was nurtured and allowed to grow. *The Times*, by all accounts, was not. I turned them down. They were flabbergasted and so were my editors at the *Inky,* who were already packing up my desk.

A year or so later *The Times* again descended. This time their attitude was, "Well, that was cute what you did, turning us down, but let's get serious."

A trusted mentor told me, "They won't ask again." So I bade goodbye to all that in Philadelphia and headed north.

These were the heady, ink-drunk days of newspaper reporting, before the internet exploded and sucked the industry dry. *The Times*, the Great Gray Lady, the Greatest Newspaper On The Face of the Earth, was busy bigfooting its way around the country, snatching up young and talented reporters of every stripe and dumping them into its newsroom. That's where I landed in the late spring of 1993. The Great Gray Viper Pit.

I can safely say that the newsroom of *The New York Times* remains, hands-down, the most neurotic, backstabbing, stomach-churning and desperately unhappy place it has ever been my misfortune to work. That includes a summer making pizza and sweating in a rat costume for Chuck E. Cheese. And several universities. So, yeah.

When I arrived at *The Times* in the spring of 1993 the paper was in the midst of a massive expansion of its metro desk. Gerald Boyd had been appointed the editor of the section a few years earlier, making him (along with Angela Dodson) one of the highest-ranking black editors at the place. The paper was also, under the dictate of the publisher Arthur Sulzberger, working hard to diversify its heretofore nearly lily-white and heavily-male staff. Since the metro desk was the point of entry for most young reporters, a significant portion of those being snatched up from other papers in those years were women and/or African-American, Latino, Asian or otherwise outside what was considered the traditional Timesman mold. The paper had also developed a reporter-training/internship program, about which many white reporters and editors made their feelings and perceptions clear.

Like I said: snake pit.

Not that I was naive about what I was walking into. Since Exeter white people had been telling me point blank that the only reason I was in their presence was because of the color of my skin. By the time I reached *The Times* that kind of nonsense no longer bothered me. For the record, here's my position on affirmative action: three hundred and fifty years for white people, fifty years for black people. Get the hell over it.

I was never stabbed in the back, mostly because my back wasn't worth dulling the knife, but I had my share of nicks and slices and I could certainly see the trails of blood running down other people's necks. Even as the anger of white men heated itself to boil at the supposed favoritism being shown to black folks plenty of white men still seemed to rise. The entire newsroom functioned as a bold and blatant star system in which some people were favored with assignments and placements and perks and some were not. People asked, "Who's your rabbi?" because it was an important question. Without one, you weren't going very far.

So a few black people got plucked and a whole lot more white men got plucked too and the rest of us all just sat in the mud and watched. Most of us black reporters didn't have a rabbi. Gerald Boyd, who had hired me and might be considered the natural candidate, told me straight out he didn't want to be the black folks' editor. That was understandable. But it also meant that when push came to vicious shove over the Jayson Blair incident poor Gerald lacked a strong, supportive constituency, while his enemies had backup to spare. The way Gerald Boyd was treated by the top editors of *The New York Times* was shameful and despicable, but it wasn't a surprise to most of the black reporters. It wasn't a surprise to me.

All of which is to say: by the start of 1995 I was miserable. My marriage was rocky. I was infatuated with a man who was not my husband and who was not, it was clear, infatuated with me. My wrists and forearms burned and ached from a nasty case of carpal tunnel I'd developed. The in-house medical professionals at the *Times* treated me with wristbands and ice and copious doses of ibuprofen but none of it helped. Some days I could barely lift my hand to the keyboard without wincing. Most of all, I hated the viper pit in which I worked and most of the vipers slithering around.

My beat was the New York City child welfare agency, an unhappy a beat as one might ever hope to hold. Writing about child welfare in any major city mostly involves attending endless, deadly-dull meetings and interviewing endless, thick-headed bureaucrats and writing frustrating, this-sucks stories overcrowding or underfunding or teen mothers who languish in foster care while their babies are removed from them or children who spend their childhoods in group homes and then at eighteen are dumped onto the street. Most of all, covering the child welfare beat means waiting for some terrible story about a child killed either by his parents or his foster parents to drop. It always drops. Within two weeks I wrote about both the brutal beating death of a 4-year-old girl by her mother and the mother's boyfriend and the terrible death of a 21-month-old girl named Queenie Baker, who arrived at her foster home in a body cast, so beaten and stunted she did not eat solid food at 10 months and who months later was dead.

This was difficult stuff.

On top of that, I woke every morning fearing that my voice was being strangled. Every day I sat in the newsroom next to one editor or the other as he/she hacked my prose into pieces and then hung them on the line to bleed. At night I went home and tried to focus on my own writing, to keep cranking out short stories and sending them out to literary magazines and editors. But after a day of battling obnoxious bureaucrats and sources, and even more obnoxious editors, I'd crawl home, crank up my clunky old word processor and just stare at the screen, empty. I was empty. When I could manage to string together a coherent sentence it just lay on the page and wheezed.

Once I gave a short story I'd written to a friend of mine in the newsroom, a guy whose writing I admired a great deal. Two days later he returned the story, sliced to within an inch of its life. It was, he said, turgid, lifeless, stilted and dull. Also the spelling sucked.

"I'm glad I don't have to pussyfoot around with you," he said. "You're tough. You can take it."

Somehow I'd gone from over-sensitive to Inhumanely Tough Black Woman with no stops in between.

If there was a single, crystalline moment of decision I don't remember it. I don't remember very much about those months at all. Looking back it feels as if I'd been drugged, as if I'd spent my days staggering through a fog. Mostly what I have is flashes: me cowering in the ladies' room, tears spiking my face. Me skulking the corners at the 42nd Street library, dreading the return to work. Me walking the streets of midtown, walking purposefully because that's the way you walk in New York, even when there's nowhere to go.F

Finally I guess God had enough. She dropped this book called *A Handbook For Constructive Living* into my hands, said, "Get moving already." That, plus the suicide of a reporter I had known back in Philadelphia lit the spark. I decided to quit.

"Are you crazy?" asked so many of my friends and colleagues I considered printing up a card with my response.

"Are you crazy?" asked my mother. She didn't care so much about the *Times* as about the steady paycheck. "You can't leave a job without having another one."

Gerald Boyd took me to lunch and looked me in the eye and shook his head sorrowfully. "If you do this, you will be making the biggest mistake of your life."

Gerald was a true believer, but even a lot of people who were miserable at *The Times* told me they could not imagine leaving it. "How would I get people to take my phone calls?" one colleague joked. I knew he wasn't really joking, and I understood. I liked having that stationery and those snazzy business cards, I liked calling people up and having them either snap to the phone or frantically avoid it, which was just as satisfying as the first. It's certainly true that for a while after I left the paper nobody would call me back.

But that just made things all the more clear to me.

Uncle Jimmy, when he was twenty-four, got on a boat across the Atlantic and fled America. He went to France, a country to which he had never been and whose language he did not speak. He did so because he doubted his ability to survive the fury of the color problem in America and because he wanted to be a writer and he knew he could not be a writer here.

"Any writer, I suppose, feels that the world into which he was born is nothing less than a conspiracy against the cultivation of his talent—which attitude certainly has a great deal to support it. On the other hand, it is only because the world looks on his talent with such a frightening indifference that the artist is compelled to make his talent important.

Uncle Jimmy fled the country to protect himself and his writing. How could I not just get on the Metro North?

M, to his great credit, said, "Quit. Quit and do what you love. We'll find a way."

At Gerald's suggestion, to calm my mother and my own latent fears of poverty rising like a ghost from the graveyard and eating me alive, I eventually decided not to quit outright, but to take an unpaid leave of absence instead. But even as I cleaned out my desk and gathered my things I knew I would not be returning to the Great Gray Lady. Come hell or high water, poverty or unemployment or unlikely riches, I had survived and I was done.

**

What I mean when I write James Baldwin saved my life is that his work has given me a kind of playbook for running this game. His essays

293

stand as a source of truth and understanding to which I return again and again and again for help in making sense of the world and all the crazy human beings in it. He was just so astonishingly smart, so perceptive and honest and courageous in the face of all the bullshit most people fluff around their lives.

When I say James Baldwin saved my life what I mean is this: he taught me what it means to be black in America and what it means to be human in this world. He taught what it means to be a writer, an artist, and he taught that I was fully and completely all of those things—black, American, writer—but a writer first and foremost. Everything flowed from that, everything stood shaped by it. Everything was explained.

He gave me a container for holding all the parts of me I could make no sense of otherwise. Why my heart overheats and my brain won't shut down and my stomach so often turns. Why the sight of an unshoveled sidewalk can fill me with hopelessness, can send me reeling home in the gloaming, wondering what point there could possibly be living in a world of people so selfish and thoughtless and self-consumed. Can really make me think of killing myself.

There are other containers for holding these parts of me, containers helpfully offered by people throughout my life. *You're too sensitive. You're too angry. You focus too much on the negative, blame everything on race. Calm down. Toughen up. Look on the bright side, look at it my way, get over it.* There are other containers, containers the world is happy to stuff you into and slam down the lid. Uncle Jimmy saved me from that.

Uncle Jimmy said, "Girl, ain't nothing wrong with you. You're a writer, that's all."

Uncle Jimmy said, "Come on into the family."

**

It took a few months after leaving *The Times* for me to find my sea legs. I had been either working or going to school or both every day of my life from the time I was fifteen to that point and it was the first time in years I woke in the morning with no particular place to go. It was strange, and guilt-inducing; I was so paranoid about strangers looking disgustedly at me as some kind of layabout welfare case that I wouldn't go out into public until after five o'clock. Which was ridiculous.

By March though I'd found my target. I began work on a novel, assigning myself a deadline of one thousand words per day. I'd done some research and discovered that the average novel was 70,000. At one thousand words a day I should have a first draft in less than three months, give or take a Sunday off. Which I did. I'd rise in the morning, see M off to work, turn off the phone (people tend not to believe you are really working when you work at home, especially on something as dubious as writing,) write until noon, break for lunch and to walk the dog, then write for several more hours that afternoon.

It wasn't blissful; writing is never precisely blissful to me. More like running straight up the side of a mountain with a croaker sack of porcupines strapped to your back and hyenas at your heels. Still, glorious when you reach the peak. I sat on my bed with my laptop and typed twee as much as I'd typed while reporting and yet my carpel tunnel disappeared.

By June I had first draft of a novel. I gave it to a friend of a friend who worked at a publishing house in NY. He gave it to an editor. She liked it and connected me to an agent. The agent sold the book. Even I recognized how criminally easy and smooth was the process. I figured if this wasn't God or the universe or something showing me I was on the right track I didn't know what was, and I went with it. (It didn't hurt that Terry McMillan had just shocked the lily-white New York publishing industry into acknowledging the astonishing fact that black women did, in fact, buy and read books..) In September, several months pregnant and with my marriage in a steady place, I sold my first novel. Happy, happy day.

That December, at the end of my leave, I strode into the newsroom and quit. In my memory it is a Norma Rae moment, me climbing big-bellied and triumphant atop my stark-clean desk and raising my hands in glee. In reality, I slid through the buzzing newsroom attracting little attention. The few friends I had on staff already knew my decision, and nobody else much cared.

During my exit interview with Joe Lelyveld, the executive editor, he sat back in his big leather chair with his arms crossed against his blindingly white shirt and his crooked little faraway smile and mused about why I might be doing such a thing.

"It's too bad things did not work out," he said, sounding bemused. "You're such a talented writer. But for some reason you just never made it into the inner sanctuary."

Now, this is a ridiculous line by any stretch of the imagination. It's like not inviting someone to a party, locking the door when they show up anyway, then asking, "Hey! What happened to you?" At the time his willful innocence infuriated me, this intentional obtuseness to structures of privilege and power and patriarchy and race and cultural hegemony not only right there in the newsroom of the Great Gray Lady but in all the news they presume to find fit to print. At the time this blindness to cultures of hegemony and power; I rolled out of the newsroom alternately wanting to firebomb the place and fall down on my knees in grateful relief at escaping it.

Then I went home and read some Uncle Jimmy and my anger fell away.

In his essay "Stranger in the Village," Uncle Jimmy wrote:

"There is a great deal of willpower involved in the white man's naiveté. Most people are not naturally reflective any more than they are naturally malicious, and the white man prefers to keep the black man at a certain human remove because it is easier for him thus to preserve his simplicity and avoid being called to account for crimes committed by his forefathers, or his neighbors..."

One thing I did as my marriage was falling apart was take up yoga. For awhile the yoga studio was the only place I could get out of my head and be in the moment. I know that sounds like a lot of touchy-feely New Age goop but it's also the simple truth. In any other form of exercise, in running or biking or jumping around in aerobics class (which I hated) my mind would keep up a steady stream of comments that had nothing to do with what was happening: I'm so lonely, but what about the children, I forgot to feed the dog, why didn't he just do X, I hope the brakes hold out another month.

But practicing yoga I had to stay completely, utterly present, because that stuff was hard. And it was from yoga that I learned that balance doesn't mean finding a spot and freezing. It doesn't mean you achieve stillness and never move again. Balance is a series of constant, incremental corrections. Balance is tension, essentially, the tension between two points.

So on it goes.

My daughter is a whipsmart, amazingly perceptive and thoughtful child who fortunately inherited her father's steady disposition. She's far from blind to the injustices and inequalities and human foibles of the world, she just refrains from taking every heart-wrenching headline personally. She believes that people are basically good and things are basically getting better and that she can help that process along. Essentially she's an optimist. God knows how that happened and God knows how grateful I am that it did. My son, on the other hand, seems to have inherited his mother's tender heart.

One day when he was four we sat in the car outside the library, waiting for his sister who was inside engaging in some children's program or such thing. It was fall and the leaves of the sugar maples and giant oaks and towering birch trees that line the streets of our small town shimmered in red and orange and gold. Who knows what I was thinking: probably wishing the stupid program would finish so I could get home and get on with the thousand other things I had to do before the day was done. Behind me, strapped into his car seat, my son chanted some song. Suddenly he lapsed into silence.

"Hey, bud, everything okay back there?" I asked after a few moments.

He said, "Mommy, sometimes the world is so beautiful it makes me want to cry."

Hand on the Bible. Four years old.

What's funny and heart-wrenching and entirely predictable, given how slowly humans evolve, is that I often catch myself trying to cajole or urge or even yell away my son's tenderheartedness. *Come on! Toughen up! Don't be so damn sensitive.* The reason is fear, of course; I'm terrified to send any tenderhearted child of mine, let alone a boy, unsheathed into this world. If anybody knows how much bruising will surely follow, how much stamping and slicing and stabbing he will have to endure it's me, and so some days I want nothing more than to wring this tenderheartedness from his body, regardless of the consequences. Better for him to hate me than to get chewed alive.

But most days I know better. Most days I know that even if such a change were possible without great damage, even if I could magically and painlessly desensitize my sensitive son, I should not. After all, he might be a writer.

And that is not such a terrible thing.

ABOUT THE AUTHOR

Kim McLarin is the author of three, critically-acclaimed novels, *Taming It Down, Meeting of The Waters* and *Jump At The Sun*, all published by William Morrow Inc. *Jump at the Sun* was chosen as a 2007 Fiction Honor Book by the Massachusetts Center for the Book. It was also nominated for a Hurston-Wright Legacy Award and chosen by the Black Caucus of the American Library Association as a 2007 Fiction Honor Book.

She is a former staff writer for *The New York Times, The Philadelphia Inquirer* and the Associated Press. Her nonfiction has appeared in *The New York Times, Glamour, The Washington Post, The Root, Slate.Com* and other publications.

She is an associate professor in the Department of Writing, Literature and Publishing at Emerson College in Boston. McLarin is also a regular commentator on *Basic Black*, Boston's historic weekly television program devoted to African-American themes, produced by WGBH in Boston.

Made in the USA
Middletown, DE
26 May 2015